COAST TO COAST GHOSTS

COAST TO COAST GHOSTS

True Stories of Hauntings Across America

LESLIE RULE

**Andrews McMeel
Publishing**

Kansas City

06 07 08 09 RDH 20 19 18 17 16 15 14 13

Photography by Leslie Rule

Library of Congress Cataloging-in-Publication Data
Rule, Leslie, 1958–
   Coast to coast ghosts : true stories of hauntings across America / Leslie Rule.
      p. cm.
ISBN-13: 978-0-7407-1866-3
ISBN-10: 0-7407-1866-5
   1. Ghosts—United States. I. Title.

BF1472.U6 R85 2001
133.1'0973—dc21
                                                            2001028970

Book design by Holly Camerlinck

For Savanna Rudberg Schreiner

I Am Ghost

I am in the shadow that creeps across your wall
And in the fingers of the wind as it tangles up your hair;
I am in the corner of the eye of the stranger lurking by;
I am Ghost.
I am in the shriek that shatters your sleep
And in the dance of the branches of the dying autumn trees;
I am in the silence and in the shouting, too;
I am Ghost.
I am in the tears weeping on your window
And reflected in the puddle in a fold between the ripples;
I am in the loneliness as she reaches for the phone,
And in the empty house, that aches for a family who will never
    return;
I am Ghost.
I am in the echo of hollow laughter gone;
I am in the rip in the wallpaper and the old patterns peeking through
And in the yellowed newspapers stacked up in the hall;
I am Ghost.
I am in the invitation forgotten in the drawer
And in the legs of the spider who lives beside the light;
I am in the rusty ring on the claw-footed tub.
I am Ghost.

                                    —Leslie Rule

Contents

CONTENTS

Foreword by Ann Rule

As a child of two writers, it was probably inevitable that Leslie Rule, my daughter, would grow up with a "silver pen"—not in her mouth but in her hand. She was born with an intense curiosity about things both seen and unseen, into a family where none of us ever said "That's impossible" and some of us believed in angels, ghosts, and good and bad spirits. Moreover, she was born in the midst of a wild storm that knocked out all the electricity in Seattle, and Virginia Mason Hospital had to operate on auxiliary power. The other mother in the labor room that day had a boy she named Daniel Boone. All the portents were right for Leslie to become a chronicler of ghost stories, except that she was *not* born with a caul.

And then again, it may have been genetic.

One of my earliest memories is of going to the cemetery with my maternal grandmother, Anna Hansen, while she put fresh geraniums on the graves of relatives I'd never known. For the adults, it was a somber occasion—but for me it was fun.

As I skipped among the tombstones, I wondered why my grandma was so sad when *I* knew everything was all right and all the people who slept beneath the green Michigan grass were now free and happy. I suspect most children know those secrets, too soon forgotten. By the time they can verbalize what they once knew, the memories are as wispy as smoke in a fierce wind.

All I can call back now of that sunny May day in the cemetery is the overwhelming sense of serenity there.

It is true that Leslie and her siblings grew up in a haunted house in a haunted neighborhood, although we never thought of it that way. There were simply things unexplainable. I never knew until I read this book just how many things my children saw that I did not. If the mass of humanity would admit the truth, I think the vast majority of us could describe at least one otherworldly visit from someone or some *thing* they could not actually describe in concrete, scientific terms. Some choose not to see what cannot be defined within the parameters of what is safe and familiar; others, like Leslie, are attuned to new dimensions and the fascinating if sometimes tragic world of those in the shadows of life.

As a writer of true-crime mostly murder cases, I work with facts that have to be supported by the very precise work of homicide detectives and criminalists who explore infinitesimal evidence in forensic laboratories. And yet, when I am writing about the life and death of particular victims, I realize I have come to know them better than anyone knew them in life. It is almost as if the victim is standing just behind my left shoulder, ready to help me find some paragraph in a police report, a certain photo among the stacks of pictures next to my desk, or a line in a statement. Homicide victims want their stories told, and they *do* help me; sometimes I just reach my hand out blindly and it touches the very piece of research that I was looking for, when common sense dictates it should have taken me hours of searching.

And because I am alone except for three dogs and five cats, I'm not at all self-conscious about calling my victim by name and whispering "Thank you."

Perhaps because I write about violent and unexpected death, I am more aware of the narrow precipice we all walk between being alive and moving on to another and, I believe, better world. I don't believe that the human soul dies when the body dies; nothing so perfect would be designed for such a short existence.

Do I believe in ghosts? Of course.

The house I live in now has its own complement of ghosts—or, rather, the land on which my house sits has its residents from another era. I live so close to Puget Sound that I am almost *in* the water. A few years after I moved here, a violent storm literally pulled three feet of beach out to sea, revealing two parallel rows of stumps. I learned there had once been a ferry dock some fifty feet out in the sound, and this was all that was left of the pilings that had once supported that dock. More than a century ago, a ferry once stopped here to pick up passengers bound for Seattle. Passengers traveled by buggy along bumpy trails and then made their way down the wooded banks to the shore of Puget Sound and waited on the dock for the boat to come. Probably thousands of people walked down the trail in my woods during that time.

In my pantry, when I am facing in the direction of the hill, I can sometimes hear a cheerful cacophony of voices. My television is off and my radio is off and there is no one on the beach. If I turn even a few degrees, the voices stop. I think I am "tuning in" to an aural slice of time out of place, listening for an instant to the sound of excited travelers headed to the dock that is no longer there.

During Prohibition in the 1920s, there was a rickety old house that stood for years where my house is now. Its player piano remained until the house was demolished, the only sign of any kind of grandeur. A "revenuer" lived here. A bachelor, he was employed by an early incarnation of the ATF (Alcohol, Tobacco and Firearms) bureau, and his job was to scan Puget Sound for boats with alcoholic cargo that violated the Volstead Act. Prohibition caused a lot of stealthy nighttime nautical traffic with hardly a light to see the passage. I'm not sure if the prohibition agent's spirit is still around, but if it is, he would approve of what I do for a living.

When Leslie was a child, I read through all the library shelves of "ghost books" avidly. My only complaint was that the stories were vague and had a sense of urban legend about them. Many of the books had the same stories, repeated endlessly, slightly changed, and I began to doubt their authenticity. When a grown-up Leslie told me she was going to research *real* ghost stories, I was enthusiastic about the project.

My daughter and I often travel to far-off cities together—but on different missions. While I am sitting in a trial, Leslie is looking for haunted houses and visiting local libraries or talking with old-timers who remember far enough back in time for her to locate the genesis of a ghost story.

One night in Wilmington, Delaware, I was interviewing a prime witness who had testified in a sensational trial, and Leslie was down in New Castle, prowling through a cemetery and reading gravestones! In San Antonio, we joined up to test an intriguing legend about a train and ghost children, aided by a reluctant Texas Ranger. The next day, I was in a trial and Leslie was looking for apparitions in the Alamo. She understands ghosts; I understand antisocial killers. It may be a strange way for mother and daughter to find the time to spend together, but for us it works.

Of course, Leslie and her husband, Kevin, have traveled to many more cities together, researching the *real* stories behind the rumors of hauntings. Leslie has always taken pictures for me to use in my books, but those were straightforward images. I was amazed at the photographs she has taken in her "ghostly" travels. Not only are her stories true, Leslie's pictures will allow readers to feel the ambiance of the homes and buildings she visited during her meticulous research.

Whether you "believe" or not, *Coast to Coast Ghosts* will let you step into that world just beyond what we see in our everyday lives. I hope you enjoy this book as much as I did, and I say that even though writer-mothers are *the* most critical readers of their own offspring's work to be found!

March 2001

Acknowledgments

Without the dozens of people who so generously shared their experiences, the pages of *Coast to Coast Ghosts* would be blank. In addition to thanking all those whose names appear in this book, I'd like to express my appreciation for my wonderful editor, Jennifer Fox.

I'd also like to thank the following for their friendship and support: Lynn Rhone; Janice Owens; Diane and Chelsea Viseth; Leonie Rodarte; Shereen Cotton; Laura Aronstein; Bill and Margaret Rudberg; Karyl Carmignani; Gloria Kempton; Teresa Grandon-Garcia; Celia Sadlou; Wendy Yadock; Janet Loughrey; Eric and Emanuela Baer; Donna Anders; Marnie Campbell; Janell Sale-Mennard; Patty St. Clair; Steve, Eleanore, Courtney, and Aubrey Repole; Allison Mcallister; Mary Kemp; Chuck Dwight, Christine Lassley; Julee Wagner; Terry Wagner; James and Harriett Clark; Theresa Zinewicz; Jan Gill; Ugo, Nancy, and Lucas Fiorante; Jerry and Jan Bergman; Earline Byers; Harmonie Rose Keene; Keith and Debby Workman; Al and Donna Smith; Lewis Argano; Diana Rhodes; Michelle Johansson; Stephanie Wilson; and Pam Ryan.

Thank you to my loyal reader, Marianne Burress, who recognized the writer in me when I was nine years old! And thank you to my agent, Sheree Bykofsky, for her endless enthusiasm.

My gratitude to my best friend and husband and favorite person on the planet, Kevin Wagner.

Introduction

When I set out to write *Coast to Coast Ghosts,* I had no intention of making myself part of the story. This book was to be a detached report of ghost sightings. I would simply interview people, report the events, and photograph charming old houses where paranormal activity was said to take place.

I did not intend to reveal the fact that I am slightly more psychic than the average person. I planned to interview renowned psychics on their perspectives of "the other side" and share their impressions of the individual hauntings I researched, but I would certainly *not* imply that I had any kind of sixth sense about the places I visited.

But the very act of going to haunted sites made me part of the story! In an effort to solve the mysteries that swirl about my subjects, I dug into the past. And as I did so, it sometimes seemed I was led by the hand to the one yellowed scrap of a document or a tired newspaper clipping that made everything clear. Vivid impressions formed in my mind, and at times it was as if a voice from the past were speaking directly to me. I "heard" some interesting remarks from people long dead.

Imagination? Perhaps. As a writer, I have a very active one. But I cannot dismiss the accuracy of past psychic experiences. For instance, I foresaw the deaths of both my father (in 1975) and my grandfather (in 1978) in dreams. It was early February when I dreamed my healthy Grandpa Stack, a retired college professor and football coach, was in the pigpen surrounded by his beloved Hampshires when he suddenly clutched his chest and fell to the ground. The dream shifted, and Grandma Sophie was hugging me so tightly I could feel her broken heart.

When I awoke, I immediately sat down and made Grandpa a valentine with a letter telling him how much he meant to me. (I did not mention my dream.) Four months later, Grandpa Stack had a fatal heart attack in the pigpen. When I saw my grandmother she wrapped me in a crushing hug and I could "feel" her heart breaking, just as in my dream.

In sharing this experience, I am not implying that I have an incredible psychic ability. I would never refer to myself as *a* psychic. Instead, I will put it more mildly and say I'm blessed with ample intuition. And this "ample intuition" has sometimes shaped the outcome of my research and made me part of the story.

I invite you, my reader, to journey with me as I travel from coast to coast and investigate haunted places. I hope you enjoy sharing the fascinating stories of the friends I've made along the way.

As this book unfolds, you will come to your own conclusions. Before we begin, consider the promises I made to myself while researching *Coast to Coast Ghosts*. I vowed to: never fabricate facts; always remember to respect the deceased—to show compassion for the poor souls who are trapped here as ghosts; and get out *fast* if a place felt truly evil!

Chapter One

Haunted Homes

When I was a little girl, I thought *everyone* lived in a haunted house. I figured a ghost was a fixture, like the bathtub and the kitchen sink. That's probably a common assumption for any kid growing up in such a place.

Des Moines, Washington, a little city on the water about ten miles south of Seattle, was settled in the late 1800s. My great-grandfather, the Reverend William John Rule, founded a Methodist church there at the turn of the century, and that's where my grandfather, John, and my father, Bill, grew up. When I was five years old, my family bought my father's childhood home from his parents.

It was a little white house with red shutters that sat on a grassy hill and overlooked the ever-changing waters of Puget Sound. It had begun as beach shack, and over the years an assortment of odd-shaped rooms were added to it. As a boy, my father had dug out the basement as a bomb shelter. His stern and often cruel father had put him to work at age eight, shoveling out the dirt below the house. He worked every day and, by the time he was eleven, little Billy Rule had dug out a thousand-square-foot area.

I'm certain it never crossed his mind that he was creating the space for his future children's bedrooms. Cool in the summer, warm in the winter, the partially underground basement was always comfortable.

But it was *creepy*.

After my parents bought the house, they worked on it for months. Every weekend we stayed there as they remodeled. Old walls came down and new ones went up as my father changed the configuration of the rooms. My mother papered and painted and laid linoleum.

While they were there alone, they would often hear the phone ring. It rang and rang and rang. And rang. But there was no phone.

They would walk to the wall where the old-fashioned telephone had once been mounted. A rectangular indentation with wires poking out was all that remained. Yet as they stood there staring at it, it would continue to ring.

Wires don't ring. Who could be calling?

My parents were not afraid, they were fascinated. When they finished remodeling, we all moved in. And there I lived until I was on my own at eighteen.

We were used to the sound of our mother typing in the basement rec room, where she had set up a corner office: *click-click click-clickety click-click-click.* But every so often, I would hear typing and open the door to sudden silence and an empty room. One of my siblings once saw a head float past the top bunk bed.

The author's home, where a confused spirit wanders.

And then there is the sobbing ghost. I'm afraid we cannot claim her as our very own, for she made her rounds throughout the entire neighborhood. She was especially attracted to a home on Sixth Avenue, one street over. The family heard her nearly every evening as dusk settled. It would begin as a faraway crying that seemed to come from the field behind their 1920s ranch-style house. But the darker it got, the closer the crying got, until the sound emanated from their cellar. Sometimes it was accompanied by the sound of jars rolling and bones crunching.

The Smiths (that really *was* their name!) were renting the house and had never ventured into the cellar. They reasoned that animals must be living in the area and were making the noises. Sandy Smith asked my mom if she would explore with her; she was afraid to go alone.

One sunny Saturday the two women got up their courage and decided to go in. They tried to get Sandy's German shepherd to escort them, but the dog stood at the threshold with her fur standing on end and refused to go another step farther. It was the exact behavior of our German shepherd, Beowulf, when it came to the room we used as a library. He absolutely would not step into that room.

My mom and Sandy went into the Smiths' cellar, expecting to find an explanation for the odd noises. The area was empty and the floor swept clean.

Night after night, the sobbing continued. Who was the ghost? Why was she so sad? I heard her once, and it was the most heart-wrenching crying I have ever witnessed. Huge gulping sobs, that grew more intense with each cry.

It was the sound of a heart breaking.

I was about twelve, and in my basement room, when I heard her.

It seemed to come from the upstairs bathroom. I assumed it was my teenage sister and hurried to find out what could be so terribly wrong. As I ran upstairs, the crying stopped.

My sister was not home. My brothers were playing outside, and my mother was in the kitchen, cheerfully making dinner.

I cannot say for certain who the phantom weeper was, but there are a couple of possibilities. One source of the haunting was discovered just recently while I was reading a book about the history of Des Moines. Decades before we moved there, someone who lived in a house on the beach died. It was the middle of winter and the horse-drawn hearse pulled the body up the road. But it was simply too icy for the horse, and its hooves slipped on the hill. So the body was buried on Cliff Avenue—in the exact spot where our mailbox would be! The unmarked grave remains there today.

I don't know the identity of the luckless dead. Could it be a woman who is unhappy with her burial plot?

The other possible source of the haunting may be caused by the reckless endeavor of Des Moines workers in 1910. My grandfather, John Rule, was ten years old that year. City workers dug out the hillside about sixty feet below the site of our future home. They were putting in the road that would eventually become Cliff Avenue.

As John and a group of boys watched, the workers' shovels struck a grisly treasure, a Native American burial site. Skeletons had been buried in a special coffin—a canoe—along with beaded necklaces and bracelets.

The boys desecrated the sacred burial ground. Whooping with excitement, they raided the grave, looting it for the jewelry grieving loved ones had once placed there. One of the boys grabbed a skull and jammed it onto a fence post.

People were shocked by the sight of the grinning empty-eyed skull staring at all who walked by. The desecration of the grave created an uproar in Des Moines, but nothing that would match the controversy if it were to happen in today's politically correct times.

The road went in, and people went about their business.

Desecrated graves are often traced as the source of a haunting. Did the horribly insensitive acts of city workers and a gang of boys prompt the phantom weeping? No one can say what tongue the sobbing woman spoke, for all we ever heard were cries. The sound of a heart breaking is the same in any language.

About twenty years after the looting of the grave, *my* childhood home was built atop the sacred burial site. No one knows how many Native Americans rest in the ground there. Our house was eventually sold to the city and torn down to make room for Overlook Park. All that remains is the sweeping water view and the lilac bush my mother planted on the bank.

Sometimes when I walk by and see the people sitting in benches there, I smile. I smile because they do not know. They do not know that they are lounging within the invisible walls of our old library, the room our dog refused to enter. And they do not know they are making themselves comfortable atop a Native American burial ground.

I wonder. Do they ever hear the sobbing?

✌❀

Though I soon learned that not everyone lives in a haunted home, I have encountered many who do—including the following people, who have agreed to share their experiences.

The Roommate

Brian Sykes has had his share of roommates. But there is one the thirty-five-year-old massage therapist will never forget.

Brian's Burien, Washington, apartment was in an old building, built in the 1940s. Weeks after moving into his bachelor pad, he began to sense he was not alone. "Odd things started happening," Brian confided. "I couldn't explain them." Each time Brian left for work, he locked Sam, his fat tabby cat, in the apartment—only to return and find Sam *outside*.

Perplexed, Brian set up elaborate barricades around his doors. Still, he would come home to find Sam waiting for him outside, and the barricades did not appear to have been touched.

Next, Brian began shutting Sam in the bathroom. "Every time I came home, Sam was outside, and all the doors and windows were shut, just as I had left them."

"I usually don't tell people that I lived in a haunted apartment," said Brian. "Most people look at you like you're weird if you admit you believe in ghosts."

But several of his friends witnessed the paranormal activity themselves when they visited one dark evening. As he entertained his company, Brian heard the distinctive sound of footsteps stomping down the hall. "We all heard it and assumed another friend had dropped by," recalled Brian. "I got up to see who it was, but the hallway was empty."

His friends exchanged nervous glances as he explained about his phantom roommate. But Brian was never afraid. "I liked living with a ghost," he admitted.

Perhaps his enthusiasm has something to do with the fact that his particular ghost did housework. Many nights Brian went to sleep, leaving a sink full of dirty dishes—only to wake up and find the dishes washed, dried, and put away.

"When I moved out, I actually invited the ghost to come with me," he confessed. Apparently, the ghost declined. "Now I have to do my own dishes," Brian complained.

Someone to Talk To

John and Kimberly Bruklis's Tampa, Florida, home does not look like a haunted house. It is a beige-brick, one-story ranch-style house where the couple live with their two sons and a menagerie of pets.

They fell in love with the house when they found it. It was the right size, and it had a big yard for kids to romp in. But shortly after they moved in, Kimberly was rearranging furniture in the master bedroom when she glanced toward the hallway and saw someone she did not expect: *a ghost.*

"He was a teenager with blond curly hair, and he wore a red shirt," Kimberly confided. "I'd never seen a ghost before." She froze as she watched the apparition float down the hall. "He stared straight ahead and didn't swing his arms like people usually do."

Unnerved, she tried to shake off the experience. But it was not the end. It was only the beginning.

"Every time I went into the bathroom in the master bedroom, I could hear what sounded like radio static coming from the towel closet," she told me.

It sounded as if a radio dial was poised between stations, allowing only fragmented words to burst out. But there was no radio in the bathroom or anywhere near. Was it a broadcast from the other side?

Six Signs of a Haunting

Think your house is haunted? The following signs *could* have logical explanations. If they occur repeatedly, it might be a sign you are not alone.

1. Pets react to something others can't see, such as growling at thin air or refusing to go in a particular room. A dog's hackles may rise.
2. People in the household are having nightmares.
3. Objects are mysteriously misplaced and often returned just as mysteriously.
4. Electrical appliances turn themselves on or off or tap water turns on or toilets flush by themselves.
5. Unexplained cold drafts or cold spots are felt.
6. Footsteps, raps on the walls, or voices are heard.

Kimberly cocked her head, listening intently as she tried to make out what the voices were saying. It was no use. The garbled voices only got more jumbled, as if many people were competing to be heard at one time.

"One day while I was standing beside the closet, it felt as if someone came up behind me and sucked the air right out of the room," she said.

Another time, as she was showering, she heard a distinctive "Hello."

"This might sound strange," Kimberly ventured, "but I didn't just hear it, I *felt* it! It was a deep muffled voice, and it felt like a mild pressure on my face."

The voices grew more persistent, and soon she was hearing them throughout the house.

"Kimberly. Are you there?"

"Kiiiimberlee!"

"Where are you, Kimberly? Hello? Kimberly?"

Once she bravely called back, "Who's there?"

The mysterious voice replied, "It's me."

She sometimes worried it was all in her head. Perhaps she was going crazy.

But she wasn't the only one in the household who was experiencing odd things. Judd, their chocolate Lab, was behaving strangely, as if he too sensed something was not right in the home. Once he even appeared to *attack* the invisible presence.

One morning, as Kimberly's toddler son, Justin, sat at the breakfast table eating his cereal, he began to giggle.

"What's so funny?" Kimberly asked.

Justin pointed a finger at the empty chair across from him. "That little boy is making faces at me!" he said.

Just an imaginary friend, Kimberly told herself.

But others were seeing things too. "My brother, Tim, stopped by when we were out and saw a woman inside," Kimberly reported.

The woman looked so much like Kimberly, Tim was sure it was her peering out at him. He confronted her later, demanding, "Why wouldn't you let me in? I *saw* you!"

"It wasn't me, Tim!" she protested. "I wasn't even home."

And then there was the evening she had company, and as they sat in the living room, a hanging lamp began to swing. As four pairs of eyes watched in amazement, the lamp gained momentum until it smashed into the wall.

Odder still was the night Kimberly and John were yanked from sleep by a sharp barking. John stumbled out of bed and found a toy dog, turning in circles as it yapped incessantly. Sleepily, he flipped it over to turn it off. But as his eyes fell on the tummy of the toy, he was suddenly wide awake. "The battery cover was missing," Kimberly said. "And there weren't any batteries in the thing! Needless to say, he threw the toy out!"

The Bruklises' ghosts seemed to have a fascination with toys. A scooter in their sons' room once raced across the floor on its own. Another time, Kimberly was in her living room when a rubber ball came soaring across the room and hit the chair. "Corey and Justin were outside playing," she said. "It came out of nowhere."

Could the paranormal activity have something to do with the trunk full of old dolls in the garage attic? Former tenants had left the trunk behind. It sat collecting dust as the antique dolls slept the years away.

Kimberly avoided the garage attic because of the odd sounds emanating from there.

"It sounded like someone clomping around in wooden shoes," she confided.

Clomp, clomp, clomp. The persistent, eerie sound turned her blood cold. Whenever she got into the car, she tried to ignore the noise. But once she became so terrified that she backed out of the garage too fast and ripped her antenna off.

John, who is much braver, climbed up the ladder and peered into the attic. The clomping ceased the instant he poked his head into the room.

Could the abandoned dolls and the mysterious noises have anything to do with the little girl ghost who'd appeared in the family's dining room to Kimberly's sister?

About a year after the Bruklises moved in, they got a call from the former owners, who said they were coming over to fetch a trunk they'd left in the attic.

Once the trunk was lugged down the ladder, the woman opened it and tenderly lifted out a doll as Kimberly watched. "These dolls belonged to my daughter," she said, as she stroked the doll's hair. "They have a lot of sentimental value for me."

"Oh?" Kimberly asked conversationally. "Is your daughter away at college?"

"No," the woman replied softly. "She died." She told the story of her young disabled daughter, who wore braces on her legs. Away at camp, the child fell from her wheelchair and sustained a head injury that led to her death.

"After they took the dolls away, we never heard the sounds in the attic again," said Kimberly.

At the same time that the clomping stopped, so did the noise of the phantom radio. Yet other paranormal activity continued. Visitors and family members saw a variety of apparitions. Maybe we're all crazy, Kimberly caught herself thinking.

Then one day, she stumbled across something in her backyard that she hoped would be a key to the paranormal activity. Then she found *another* and *another*. Would she finally have an answer to what had happened at her home?

About that time, she saw the apparition of a brown-haired boy of about nine years old in her dining room, near the spot where her sister had seen the little girl. Justin was now old enough to express himself well, and he surprised Kimberly when he told her he remembered the ghost of the boy who had made faces at him at the breakfast table. "He described the same boy I saw," said Kimberly.

My Psychic Friend

While Nancy Myer willingly shed light on some of the mysterious cases in *Coast to Coast Ghosts,* she is better known for her work with police departments.

Nancy's ability to crack difficult crimes is so well documented that she receives up to twenty requests a day for help. "About ninety percent of the time, I'm able to provide the police with new information," said Nancy, coauthor of *Silent Witness,* a book about her abilities.

Retired Delaware State Police Colonel Irvin Smith validated the claim. "I've utilized Nancy's gift on many occasions," he told me. "It's simply phenomenal what she's able to re-create about a crime."

Armed with only the victim's name, the date of a crime, and photos of the scene, Nancy usually "sees" the killer and senses the victim's thoughts at the time the crime was committed. "It's like watching a movie running in my head," she explained.

The Pennsylvania mother of three grown children went public with her ability in 1975 because of her sympathy for the mother of a boy who was missing after a boating accident. "I thought that if my son were out on the marshes, I'd want somebody to help him in any way they could."

Down at the riverbank, she stared at the water. "I sensed that the boy had been swimming away from the houseboat, but that his leg became tangled in some kind of rope." She also sensed that he was disoriented, couldn't see, and headed for shore using his sense of smell. She accurately predicted where the teenager's body would be found. His family later confirmed that he was practically blind without his glasses.

Despite her accuracy, Nancy had to be coaxed by police to begin working with them on a regular basis. She prefers to study photos of crime scenes rather than actually visit the site. The latter is too intense. "It feels like a gorilla sitting on my chest," she explained.

Once a pair of skeptical cops tricked Nancy into going to a house where an elderly woman had been murdered. They didn't think she would catch on—until she got out of the squad car. Overwhelmed with the horror of what had happened, Nancy began to scream, "I can see her being stabbed!" The sheepish rookies were later bawled out by Colonel Smith.

Though she is internationally respected for her unique skills, Nancy is the first to admit that she is not always right—just 90 percent of the time!

While the mystery may be fascinating to an outsider, it was unsettling for the Bruklis family. Determined to find the root of the haunting, Kimberly approached a neighbor. "Do you know anything about the history of this area?" she asked tentatively.

The woman's eyes lit up with interest. "Why?" she asked, a little too quickly.

Kimberly was noncommittal.

"Have you seen ghosts?" the neighbor surprised her by asking.

When Kimberly admitted she had, the neighbor broke into tears of relief. *Her* family had been seeing them too. She had urged her husband and children to keep it secret, for she feared others would think they were crazy.

"I've been finding these things in my backyard—" began Kimberly.

"I'll be right back!" said the neighbor, and she rushed home, returning seconds later with an object identical to the ones Kimberly had found.

It was time to take the investigation further.

When library research yielded little information, Kimberly grew frustrated. With her blessing, I sought help from someone who just might have answers.

Internationally renowned psychic Nancy Myer had no prior knowledge of Kimberly before she studied a small color snapshot of the Bruklis home.

"Many people have died here," Nancy stated, the instant she laid eyes on the picture. "And many of them are still here. There's a battlefield behind your house," she told Kimberly. "Walk about fifteen feet to the left of your backyard and you will be standing right—"

"Kimberly," I interrupted. "Tell Nancy about what you found!"

"We've been finding old cannonballs in the backyard," said Kimberly.

"I'm not surprised," said Nancy. She went on to describe some of the spirits she sensed at the Bruklis home. "There's an older woman who once lived on the site," she said. "She's still here because she loved the place so much. She loved to sit and watch the birds. I'm seeing Rose. Her name might be Rose. Or it could mean that she liked roses.

"Another ghost," Nancy continued, "was a very young woman with long, thick dark hair. Her infant died of a disease in the middle of an epidemic. The disease was passed to the baby during birth. The mother was so distraught that she drowned herself. She's still here looking for her baby."

"What about a little girl?" I asked. "Do you sense a little girl?"

"Yes," said Nancy. "She's obsessed with skipping. I don't know why, but she is obsessed with learning to skip."

"Do you see something about her feet?" I prodded.

"Yes."

We told Nancy about the mysterious clomping and asked if that was the source of the sound. Was the little ghost girl in braces trying to skip?

Nancy confirmed that she was and told us about *another* girl. "This one is twelve and had polio. She died in the hospital."

"Kimberly saw the ghost of a boy," I said. "Can you pick up anything on him?"

"He's about nine and he has brown hair?" asked Nancy.

"That's him!" said Kimberly.

"He loved the area," said Nancy. "He was a little archaeologist and was always digging things up."

Nancy went on to say that Kimberly was very psychic. "But you're not very comfortable with the idea," she added.

"That's true," said Kimberly. "I don't know what to think about seeing and hearing all these things."

"The ghosts are excited because they finally have someone who can hear them after all these years," explained Nancy.

"I'm so relieved," said Kimberly. "I was afraid I was going crazy."

Kimberly Bruklis is definitely *not* crazy. She's a compassionate person with the proverbial "third eye" and, it seems, a third ear too. Put three and three together and you've got six, as in *sixth sense*.

No, Kimberly is not crazy. She's simply someone who can see and hear the ghosts. She is someone for them to talk to.

The day after the reading with Nancy, Kimberly got a letter from a paranormal investigator who is also psychic. He wrote that he was picking up on a spirit named Rose, the same name Nancy mentioned.

We also noted that the mourning ghost Nancy described had the same long dark hair as Kimberly. Was this who Tim saw in the window of the Bruklises' empty house?

"I Know You Are Cold"

Dave and Judy Pugh's three sons have grown up and moved away. But the Elkton, Maryland, schoolteachers are not alone in their charming century-old home. Though they, themselves, have never seen their "boarder," they knew she is there. "We call her the Spirit," said Dave, adding that she is welcome to stay as long as she likes.

Almost thirty years ago, they had their first inkling of the Spirit's presence. Their oldest son, Jonathan, just a year old, was playing in the kitchen with pots and pans. When he rolled a lid down the hallway, Judy went to retrieve it, only to find it had vanished.

Had it rolled beneath the sofa? Behind the door? Or had it rolled into the other side? That's a good guess, for all these years later the pan lid is still missing.

Nearly three decades of sharing their home with the Spirit have taught the Pughs a few things about her. They know she is nurturing, friendly, and tidy. She is the quintessential hostess, who thrives on people and parties. She loves the home they share as much as they do. And she has a penchant for pretty things and sometimes cannot keep from borrowing them.

Judy discovered that fact when she purchased a dress and a matching purse and shoes for a special event. She carefully placed the new things in her bedroom closet. But when she reached for the purse, it was gone.

Despite a thorough search, she could not find it and finally chose a different handbag. Puzzling over the mystery, she went to the event. She checked the closet again upon returning home, but the purse had not turned up.

When Judy was getting ready for bed that night, she opened her closet. The purse was back, hanging beside the dress.

Then there was the time Judy's favorite pearl earrings disappeared. "She always kept them in the same place," Dave explained. "We questioned the boys, but none of them knew anything about it. Of course, that was in the days before boys wore earrings." The very next day, the pearl earrings reappeared, nestled in their usual spot.

Though they have yet to see her, the Pughs know the Spirit is a lovely blond with a perpetual smile. I wish *I* could have seen her during my visit to the Pugh house, but only three people have been so lucky.

In the mid 1970s, Judy and Dave were hosting a dinner party when one of their guests (who happened to be psychic) announced she had just seen a tall, slender woman walk up the inside staircase and vanish. The apparition wore a black chiffon skirt with an apron. Her fine blond hair was swept atop her head. "I sense she likes parties and people," the guest said, as the others listened in fascination.

The psychic also guessed that the Spirit had been a Follies dancer and the house had been built for her. This later assumption has yet to be proven, but the physical description matches those of later witnesses.

The second sighting occurred at Thanksgiving of 1987, when relatives were staying over. One of them, Louise, a thirty-something woman (who had never heard one word about the haunting), awoke in the night.

Suddenly, she sensed someone standing over her. She rolled over to see a tall blond woman in a black chiffon dress gazing down at her. "I know you can see me," said the apparition. "I know you can hear me. I know you are cold." And the Spirit gently pulled the covers up over Louise's shoulders.

Though the gesture was kind, it shocked Louise so much she barely slept for the rest of the night.

A friendly spirit tucks guests in at this Elkton, Maryland, home.

Another decade passed before Judy's sister, Sue, met the Spirit. Like Louise, Sue had not heard the Pugh ghost stories. "We kept it quiet because we didn't want to discourage visitors," explained Dave.

It was the middle of the day. Sue walked upstairs toward the guest room where she'd been staying and then paused, sensing eyes upon her. She turned to see a tall blond woman smiling at her. The stranger wore a black chiffon dress with a white apron. As Sue watched, the woman continued up to the third floor.

Sue entered her room to find her belongings moved. It was as if someone had been tidying up.

Psychic Nancy Myer studied a photograph of the Pugh house and described a tall buxom woman who, she said, was once the matron of the house. "She is obsessed with taking care of the home," said Nancy.

Though Nancy seemed to pick up on the apparition seen by the Pugh's guests, she differed on one point. She believes the ghost is an older woman with *white* hair, not blond. When it comes to ghost sightings, Nancy said, "Many people get white and blond confused."

Déjà Vu

In 1995, my husband and I moved into a house so much like my childhood home that it was like a déjà vu.

The 1905 house was built by a sea captain. It sat on a hill overlooking Puget Sound, about a mile down the beach from where I grew up. *And* it, too, was haunted. Now, lest readers think it too coincidental that I should live in two haunted homes, let me point out that I have lived in twenty-four places in my lifetime. The vast majority did *not* include ghosts.

The Zenith, Washington, home had been owned and occupied by the folks who ran the little grocery store where I shopped for penny candy as a child. The wife, Margaret, was a sweet lady who had died a few years before. Johnny lived on there without her for a few years; he loved the sprawling yard with its dozens of flowering shrubs. But one day he fell in the tub and fractured his hip. He was stuck there for several days, unable to reach the phone. When his worried son called neighbors, they broke down the door and found him. He moved to a nursing home and was pleased to learn that old friends bought his beloved home.

Snooty neighbors stopped by to welcome us and ask when we were planning to "gut" the house. We had no such plans. We loved the character of the place, with its well-worn creaking floors, leftover antique carpet, and rustic kitchen cabinets.

I especially loved the wallpaper in the entryway. You could literally peel back a corner and flip through the decades like pages in a book. Layer after layer of wallpaper peeked through: 1980, 1970, 1960 . . .

When a flowery design of fifty years before was revealed, I almost felt as if I had stepped back into time.

Our first night there, we slept in sleeping bags on the living room floor. I was sound asleep when Kevin woke me up. "Listen!" he said. "What's that noise?"

It sounded like something clanging on pipes, intermingled with phantom footstep.

"Go back to sleep," I told him. "It's just ghosts."

As the months went by, we often heard inexplicable noises. The most common sounded like a china cabinet crashing down. We'd run around the house, trying to discover what the cats could have knocked over, but we never found anything.

Haunted as a Matter of Law

In July 1991, the New York State Supreme Court's Appellate Division declared a Nyack house to be haunted. In the 3–2 decision, they cleared the way for the former buyers to recoup their $32,000 down payment.

The old riverfront house with its charming wraparound porch and three-story tower was not what the buyers had bargained for. When they found they could not live with the home's extra features, they sought legal assistance.

"As a matter of law, the house is haunted," the State Supreme Court ruled.

Once, in the middle of the night, Kevin got up for a snack and heard a sharp rapping on the wall over the refrigerator. And on an early spring afternoon, I heard the distinct sound of someone clipping hedges. I followed the snipping noise to our voluminous hedge but saw no one. I walked around it, sure I would find a neighbor crouched there with clippers. The sound abruptly stopped. There was no one in sight.

I learned afterward that Johnny had died weeks earlier in the nursing home. I figured he was getting an early start on the yardwork.

We saw no ghosts at the sea captain's house, but we continued to hear things. The oddest moment came when we bought an old dining room table and had to remove the front door to get it inside. Immediately after, I was vacuuming beside the missing door, when someone *screamed* in my ear!

It was not in my head. It was loud. It was angry. And it was familiar. I had heard that same irritation many years before.

I was about eight years old and buying candy for my little brothers at Johnny's grocery store. I was always in awe of the mechanical counter that moved when you put the merchandise on it. Of course, nearly all grocery stores have them today, but Johnny's store was the first place I'd ever seen one.

Johnny and Margaret were always extremely nice to us, but on this day Johnny must have been in a bad mood. Some of the penny candy slipped down under the moving counter and he had a bit of a temper tantrum. He waved his hand around and yelled, "Well, let's just put it *all* down there!"

He had had cancer in his mouth that affected his speech, giving an odd note to his voice. When he yelled that day, it was a distinctive sound that I never forgot. I'm sure he didn't intend to be harsh, but I was a sensitive child and was absolutely crushed. I remember carrying a heavy sadness with me for the rest of the day.

So when I heard the ghostly voice yelling in my ear all those years later, I recognized it. It was him. And this time he was mad because we took the door down!

When Nancy Myer studied a photograph of the house, I expected her to pick up on Johnny. She surprised me when she said, "I hear a woman crying."

The only place I'd heard ghostly crying was in my childhood home, a mile up the beach.

"There's a woman here who is very, very confused about where she is supposed to be," said Nancy. "She is wandering around, desperate to find a child. The child was abducted and never seen again. I'm not sure if she was the girl's mother, but she was responsible for the child."

"How old was she?"

"About four or five."

"What happened to her?" I asked, wincing.

"She was abducted by a pedophile. He killed her and buried her in the mountains."

"What year?"

"Nineteen-sixteen," she replied decisively.

Nancy then brought up Johnny's ghost. "He knows he's dead," she said, "but he can't let go. He doesn't want to leave because he loves the place so much."

By the time this book is in print, the old sea captain's home will be torn down. The yellow house will turn to dust, the book of wallpaper closed forever.

I hope Johnny won't be too disappointed in us for selling his home. Perhaps he will let go and move on. When he does, I hope he finds the sad guilt-ridden ghost and helps her find the light.

Chapter Two

THE LITTLEST GHOSTS

Casper, the friendly ghost! The friendliest ghost we know. . . .

I knew the words to *that* song when I was just a toddler. My friends and I sat cross-legged in front of the black-and-white television, eyes wide as we watched the adventures of the child ghost who did not want to scare people.

He only wanted to play.

It was, of course, just a cartoon. Yet it captured the real-life predicament of thousands of little lost spirits.

Children are not supposed to die. They have so much more unfinished business than their elders. Still so many trees to climb, birthday candles to blow out, and adventures to have! Is it any wonder that so many can't move on?

I've researched many reported cases of innocent ones who are caught between life and death, unable to give up playtime to go beyond. Here is a sampling from my files on the littlest ghosts.

The Last Picture Show

Lauren Griego, business manager of the Albuquerque, New Mexico, KiMo Theater, led me through this beautiful historic building. I followed her down a long corridor to an area backstage. "This is Bobby's shrine," she explained, as I studied a wall adorned with children's toys and snacks. The plastic Superman, dusty yo-yo, matchbox cars, and dozens of hardened doughnuts were all offerings made to appease a sometimes naughty little ghost who is believed to make mischief without these bribes.

"We like our little ghost," said Lauren, who has never witnessed any of his shenanigans but remains open to the idea that the KiMo Theater is haunted. She acknowledges the fact that many people believe the child who died there in a terrible accident now haunts the theater. The boy's family is uncomfortable with the idea. Out of respect for them, Bobby's last name is left out of this account.

Of course, no one knows for certain who the ghost is. One unconfirmed report says a dancer took a fatal tumble from the theater stage, and it is *her* restless spirit who causes the mischief there.

But Bobby's tragic story was well documented. A 1951 summer-morning issue of the *Albuquerque Journal* reported the sad news:

A six-year-old boy was killed and at least seven persons injured Thursday afternoon when a hot-water heater exploded in the lobby of the KiMo theater. . . .

In an odd sequence of events, the youngster ran *toward* his death. He and two friends, seven-year-old Ronald and eleven-year-old Lou Ellen, were settled in their balcony seats watching *This Is America,* a prelude to the feature film Abbott and Costello's *Comin' 'Round the Mountain,* when Bobby was apparently frightened by a noise on the screen. He leapt up and dashed down the aisle, with attentive Lou Ellen chasing him. Bobby rounded the corner—straight to his fate.

Beneath the stairs, an eight-gallon electric heater provided hot water for the concession stand cleanup. On this day, something went horribly wrong. The heater exploded as Bobby approached. It was as if a bomb went off. Chunks of plaster rocketed across the theater.

Lou Ellen grabbed her little brother, Ronald, along with a frightened toddler she noticed standing lost and bewildered amid the chaos. She shepherded the children outside, still frantically searching for Bobby.

Shock waves rolled over the city as word of the disaster spread. Among the injured was a man who lost an eye. But the most horrifying news, broadcast over the radio, shattered the sunny day. The corpse of an unidentified boy waited in the morgue for his unsuspecting parents to claim him.

When Lou Ellen's mother rushed to the theater, she felt a surge of relief at the sight of her children. Then she looked into her daughter's wide eyes and her heart sank.

"I can't find Bobby!" Lou Ellen cried.

Just an hour before she had dropped the three youngsters off at the movies; now she had the sad task of identifying the body of her children's playmate.

Half a century later, KiMo showcases spectacular stage performances and wonderful musical extravaganzas, but it is also known as the playground of a little lost ghost.

In 1988, Tony Marsh, KiMo's technical director, told a reporter for the *Albuquerque Journal* how a hungry little ghost helped himself to doughnuts left in a box on the table. "I would be the first one here and the last one to leave, and *I* didn't take them," he insisted.

On a lark, crew members began to tie doughnuts against the back wall. When *A Christmas Carol* was performed there, the New Mexico Repertory Theater's crew cleared away the stale doughnuts.

"The night of the tech rehearsal before the first performance, everything that could go wrong, went wrong," said Tony. "Light cues didn't work. Sound cues didn't work. Actors were walking into each other. It was a total disaster."

The stage manager put some doughnuts backstage the next day and the little ghost was apparently appeased, for the preview night went smoothly!

The situation was repeated countless times over the years as new productions took over the theater, neglected to leave treats, and met disaster. As soon as a treat was left on Bobby's wall, all would go well again.

Bobby seems to have a kindred spirit at the Strand Theater in Key West, Florida. Today the ornate historical building houses a *Ripley's Believe It or Not* museum, where employees have long suspected a child's ghost is playing tricks on them.

When the building shuts down at night and workers are preparing to leave, the sound system often comes on by itself. Objects are inexplicably moved. And the wax head of one of the displays is constantly removed.

I dove into the archives at the local library and discovered that on July 6, 1934, twelve-year-old Jack Perez met a horrible death in the theater. The boy had gone to work with his father, Manuel, the projectionist. The projector caught fire, trapping Jack behind a wall of flames.

Onlookers held back the frantic father when he tried to leap into the fire to save his son. They knew it was too late.

Some believe that, after Manuel's death years later, his spirit joined his son at the theater, where together they enjoy playing tricks on the living.

The ghost of a boy killed at Key West's Strand Theater delights in playing tricks on employees.

This dollhouse is a replica of the haunted Key West museum, Wrecker's House, where several little girls who died here can be heard playing marbles.

Mystery Children

Some cases of ghostly children remain unsolved mysteries. Despite diligent digging in the old archives, the answers are frustratingly elusive—such as in the case of the little girl ghost who once resided with Chad Howard.

When he was nine years old, Chad and his family moved into a charming yellow house in Owensboro, Kentucky. Two stories tall, with a bedroom for each of the four kids, it seemed perfect. And it *was*—for two years. "Then we remodeled the bathroom," said Chad. "That's when strange things started happening."

Chad's mother, Darlene, was taking a nap in her upstairs bedroom as her baby son slept in the next room. She woke to see her daughter, Jennifer, rushing through the room toward the baby's room. "Stop," she called softly, "you'll wake the baby! Come back here!"

The child did as she was told and turned and walked back into the room.

"Come here, honey," said Darlene as she watched her daughter—or rather the little girl she *assumed* was her daughter. For Darlene was not wearing her glasses; she saw only the blurry image of a girl. She could tell the girl stared back at her, standing rigid and zombielike. Thinking Jennifer was being naughty, she sternly said, "I told you to come here."

The girl took off running.

Later in the day, Darlene scolded Jennifer. "Shame on you! You know better then to run away from me," she said.

"What?" the bewildered girl replied. "I didn't do that!"

An aunt confirmed that Jennifer had been sound asleep at the time. It couldn't have been her.

Chad has just *one* sister. So who did his mother see?

"After that, weird little things started happening," he confided. "Lights would turn off and then come on as you approached the light switch, or not come on until you left the room. Some of the kitchen utensils hanging on the wall would swing, while others beside them stayed perfectly still. Even if you stopped one from swinging, it would start again the instant you let it go."

Then there was the odd behavior of Angel, the family's black schnauzer mix. While in Darlene's room, she stared up at the ceiling and cocked her head, her big brown eyes inquisitive. She stood on her hind legs, her furry paws waving as she did her begging trick. Chad watched, incredulous, as the pooch pantomimed shaking hands.

One evening, as Chad, his younger siblings, and two cousins sat around the dinner table, a glowing sphere moved from the living room and flashed past them. The startled children watched as it disappeared into the bathroom.

"Did you see *that?*" Jennifer asked excitedly. The others nodded.

Was it the little girl's spirit, taking on another form? She was indeed haunting the home, for Chad saw her apparition too.

"I saw her just once," he said. "She walked from the kitchen into the living room while I watched TV late one night. She stared at me as she walked across the room."

The ghost was transparent, as if she were a slide, projected into the room. Yet she was three-dimensional. "She had long hair and wore a long gown," said Chad.

The ghost ducked behind the television and vanished.

"When we finally moved away, we didn't tell the new occupants about the sightings," Chad explained. "A few years later, I learned that they moved out of the house and had a priest exorcise it. When I told my mother, she contacted the people we had sold the house to. They spoke of seeing a little girl ghost throughout the house and said that after a while it became violent. They decided to leave when the husband awoke one morning to see a demonic creature standing over the bed. He said he couldn't move or yell until the creature noticed he was awake and disappeared."

Who was the little girl who haunted the Kentucky home? Did a child die in there?

As I write this, Chad and I both continue to research the house's past. For now, the answer remains a mystery.

Another mystery still waits to be solved at the Casa de Benavidez in Albuquerque, New Mexico. Paul Benavidez described one night he awoke to the eerie singing of children. "It sounded like ring-around-the-rosy," he told me.

In the living quarters above his family's restaurant, Paul strained his ears as he tried to figure out where the singing was coming from.

He got up and searched the magnificent adobe building. On this night, nothing was out of place. But this is not always the case. Whoever is haunting the Casa de Benavidez sometimes leaves a mess.

Over four decades ago, Rita and her husband, Paul Benavidez Senior, began to work on their dream of opening a restaurant. Both are creative chefs, and Rita has always been known for her nurturing nature, a trait that is a plus for those who deal with hungry people. The team was a success, and they eventually moved their business to the huge turn-of-the-century house that was called the Newlander Addition after the builder who constructed it.

Rita and Paul and their four children make their home upstairs so they can be close to their thriving restaurant. The authentic Mexican food served in the grand atmosphere attracts crowds of diners, including regulars who love to eat on the patio beside the soothing waterfall.

When the last customer has left, the tables are wiped clean, and the hardworking family puts up their aching feet, they realize they are not alone.

Paul Junior shook his head as he told of falling silverware, high-pitched giggles, and the inexplicable sound of little feet running. Then there is the odd behavior of the computer that servers use to produce their order tickets. "I've stood across the room and watched it operate by itself," he said, describing how the tickets fly out as if possessed by a will of their own.

Rita Benavidez is not frightened by the mischievous presence. Her face was pained yet thoughtful when someone suggested that the spirits may actually be her two young sons who died years before they opened the restaurant. "There *is* something here, but I don't know what it is," she admitted.

Whoever the ghosts are, they are extremely naughty. Paul Junior described the time a cook was staying with them and awoke in the middle of the night to shrill giggling. As the startled man sat up, a chair suddenly sailed across the room and landed on him.

Then there was the day an employee had just finished scouring the women's rest room. The restaurant was closed, and she was the only one there. She went back to get her cleaning supplies and got a shock. The toilet paper had been unraveled and rolled all over the room, draped over the sinks and other fixtures like a garland.

Despite long hours of research, I was not been able to find any records of children who died on or near the premises. The Benavidez family, however, does not mind sharing the restaurant with the mischievous little ghosts—especially considering the possibility that they may be family.

Johnnie's Playground

The St. James Hotel in Cimarron, New Mexico, was once a hangout for the Wild West's most famous gunfighters. Jesse James, Annie Oakley, Wyatt Earp, Kit Carson, Buffalo Bill—they were all known at the St. James.

In the late 1800s, the rectangular-shaped adobe building on the Santa Fe Trail was a place where travelers stopped when they were tired, hungry, and thirsty. There they found comfortable accommodations in hotel rooms equipped with their own sinks, a rare luxury in that era. The hotel's proprietor served delectable meals. Indeed, owner

Henri Lambert had previously been Abraham Lincoln's cook!

As for their thirst, they could quench that in the St. James Hotel's saloon. And quench they did! And quench and quench and quench. Sarsaparilla was *not* the beverage of choice. To this day the saloon's ceiling is scarred with bullet holes, from gunshots by rowdy customers.

It must have been a little unsettling for Mrs. Lambert, who lived on the premises with her husband and children. Buffalo Bill and Clay Allison were drinking in the bar the night she

The St. James Hotel, where one little ghost never stops playing.

gave birth to her son Fred. (Buffalo Bill eventually taught the boy to shoot and nicknamed him Cyclone Dick.)

Prostitutes once took over the upstairs floor, and apparently business was good. Gunfights were common. No less than twenty-six men met their fate at the St. James. Those who knew the reasons for the deadly disputes are, of course, long gone. We can only guess at the reasons. Love? Lust? Money? These ingredients were available at the St. James. Add alcohol, and you've got a volatile cocktail.

One psychic who visited the hotel in the 1980s surmised that the place was haunted by a gambler who had won the hotel in a poker game. The winner, she said, was killed before he took owner-ship and is the entity who haunts the hotel's infamous Room 18.

Though often reported as fact, no documentation has been found to support this.

What has been documented, however, are hundreds of reported paranormal experiences. Employees and customers tell of lights turning themselves on, objects vanishing into the floor, and sightings of a small blond figure, dubbed the Imp.

Poltergeists?

Poltergeists, German for *noisy ghosts*, have long been associated with households with children. Bucking beds, inexplicable knocking, and items thrown about have often been categorized as poltergeist activity—mischief caused by a naughty spirit. But the latest theory by leading paranormal investigators suggests that a poltergeist is not a ghost after all. Today it is thought that such activity is caused by the mind of an agent—particularly an adolescent. Without even realizing what they are doing, troubled youths use their psychokinetic (mind over matter) ability to affect the environment around them.

Clues it is a poltergeist:

1. Objects are tossed about by an unseen force.
2. Mysterious knockings, rappings, and other noises are disturbing the household.
3. There is an adolescent in the home—particularly a *girl*.
4. The teenager in question is experiencing emotional turmoil.
5. The paranormal activity stops when the teen is absent.
6. Apparitions are usually not seen.

No one is allowed in the hotel's most haunted area, Room 18. The present owner insists that disaster strikes immediately after anyone spends the night there.

My friend and fellow writer, Cheri Eicher, and I arrived after dark on a September evening. We stepped into the lobby and felt something watching us. Glancing up, we saw the heads of long-dead deer and moose, who stared back glassy-eyed.

Michele, the exhausted combination bartender and front desk clerk, greeted us and requested that we save our questions till morning. Winding down from an eighteen-hour shift, she was not up for talking about ghosts.

We followed her up the staircase and down a long hall toward the Mary Lambert room. Before we reached the door, it drifted open with such a foreboding creak I was sure it was a special effect. But no, Michele was just as surprised as we were. "This door is not supposed to be unlocked!" She sounded shaken. "And the light is not supposed to be on! She must have known you were coming."

Cheri and I glanced at each other. *"She?"*

"She must mean Mary," whispered Cheri.

Mary's room was charming but small, so we helped Michele move the bed to make room for a cot. As Michele exited, she stopped short. She pointed a trembling finger across the hall to the Katie Lambert room. "That door wasn't open a minute ago!" she exclaimed. "And the light wasn't on!"

We stared at the wide-open door. We all thought it had been shut a moment before. But then, we were all tired. Perhaps our minds were playing tricks on us.

As Michele made a hasty retreat down the hall, Cheri said, "The room smells good—like perfume."

Though the room was named for Mary, it had actually been the prostitutes' quarters. A phantom perfume has often been reported there. After dropping off our luggage, we visited the saloon downstairs. Michele played a video of a string of TV programs that featured the St. James's haunting, including *Unsolved Mysteries*. They showed a reenactment of a sighting by a former employee and depicted the ghost as a gargoyle-faced boy about nine.

"I wonder if a child died here," I said to Cheri.

When bedtime arrived, I took the cot, and I said, as Cheri settled into the bed, "I want to see a ghost. If something happens tonight, wake me up."

Cheri shivered and pulled the quilt up to her chin. "Okay," she promised. "But if *you* see anything, don't wake *me* up!" With the black night pressing against the window, she was losing her enthusiasm. Though a couple of rooms were rented in a new adjacent structure, we were the only guests in the old building, and Cheri was afraid.

I soon fell into my usual deep sleep. Cheri slept too but suddenly woke up late in the night. As she lay in bed, she faced the transom window over the door. The door to the Katie Lambert room, across the hall, still stood open, and its light shone through into our room. Cheri was comforted by the light—until it suddenly went out. *Who turned it off?* She held her breath, listening for footsteps. Nothing.

She could not get back to sleep. An hour had passed when she heard footsteps outside the door. "Leslie!" she called. "Wake up!"

"Orumfh," I replied sleepily, and pulled the pillow over my head.

For long minutes, Cheri listened as someone paced outside our door in the creaking hall. Then, about 3 A.M., I felt a soft caress on my cheek, as if a little hand had patted me. Suddenly I was wide awake. When Cheri described the earlier events, I said, "The light probably just burned out."

I crossed the hall and found the light switch in the off position. I flipped it on. How could it have turned itself off? "Maybe someone is playing a joke on us," I reasoned. "Let's see if I can walk without making noise." I stepped lightly on the sides of the hall. No matter what I did, the floor creaked and groaned with each movement.

Cheri had heard the footsteps an hour after the light went out. Had someone turned off the light and then stood there for a full hour before walking away?

Unlikely.

When the golden morning light sifted through our window, I said, "Let's go to the cemetery. I think we'll find answers there."

"We don't have much time," Cheri reminded me. "You have a plane to catch."

The old Cimarron Cemetery was on a hill, a mile from the hotel. I gazed over the sprawling resting place at the hundreds of stones and said, "I want to find the Lambert family plot."

"It will take forever to find it!" said Cheri. Remarkably, my feet took me straight to the spot, and I found myself gazing through an iron fence at the Lamberts' graves: CHARLES FRED LAMBERT, 1887–1971. KATIE HOOVER LAMBERT, 1886–1964. CATHERINE HOOVER, 1854–1940. BABY LAMBERT, September 2, 1911. JOHNNIE LAMBERT, son of HENRI AND MARY, August 1889–February 23, 1892.

"I found him!" I called to Cheri. She rushed over. "Johnnie is the little boy ghost. He was two and a half when he died."

"He's too young," said Cheri. "*Unsolved Mysteries* showed him as an older boy."

"They may have taken creative license," I argued. "I'll ask the guy who saw him."

I was able to contact the eyewitness's father, who told me, "My son doesn't like to talk about it. But I can tell you exactly what he told me." He described the morning his son had been cleaning the hotel when he spotted a child sitting on the bar, spinning a bottle. Assuming the boy was a guest, he approached him and said, "You're not supposed to be down here. You better go back to your room."

As he got closer he noted that the child wore a long white gown and his blond hair trailed to his shoulders. The child glanced up at him. Half his face was horribly disfigured, as if burned. As

Though Johnnie Lambert was buried here, his spirit does not rest.

he watched in shock, the boy jumped off the counter and disappeared *into* the floor.

"How old was the boy?" I asked.

"My son said he was a *little* boy."

"A toddler?"

"Yes."

I sent away for the death records for little Johnnie and the unnamed baby buried beside him and waited for impatient weeks. Had Johnnie died in a fire?

Unfortunately, no records could be found for either.

I consulted Nancy Myer, who "read" photos of the St. James I provided. She had never heard of the hotel and had no idea of so much as the location.

The Three Little Ghosts
of the St. James

According to psychic Nancy Myer, Cimarron's St. James Hotel is home to three little ghosts. Johnnie, "a barrel of mischief," she explained, is responsible for most of the paranormal activity at the hotel. His mother has tried for many decades to get the spirited toddler to move on with her. "He's happy," said Nancy. "He's having a good time." But his reluctance to leave his earthly playground also prevents Mary Lambert from moving on.

Nancy's reading of a St. James photo revealed that two little girl ghosts also reside there. "They died of diphtheria," she said. "It was probably in the late 1800s." She described their long hair in sausage curls—one a blond, the other a brunette. Their names might be Andrea and Melody, with a last name that is either Simple or Sample, Nancy told me. The older girl is twelve and the younger is nine. Two boys in the family also became sick. They survived, but the younger one was nine months old and his health was weakened for the rest of his life.

"Their father may have been a teacher," Nancy added. "He was very good at math." The polite girl ghosts were strictly raised and are shocked by the toddler's naughty manners. "The girls are aware of Johnnie," she said, "but they don't approve of him."

As for the gunfighters who lost their lives there, Nancy said that though they may appear sometimes and are quite capable of playing jokes on the living, they spend most of the time in caves in the hills, where they felt safer in their lifetimes.

Nancy took one look at the first photo and stated, "There have been over twenty murders here."

"Yes!" I said. "You're right."

"It was once a brothel," she added.

"The top floor," I replied. "What can you tell me about a child who died there."

"Which one?" she asked. "There are *nine*."

"Tell me about the little boy. He was two and a half."

Nancy laughed. "That child had more energy than any one child has a right to."

"Do you have a sense of his name?"

"It's something like Joseph or Joe."

"Close. It was Johnnie," I said. "Is his face disfigured?"

"He was burned. Someone was carrying fried food in a big pot. He ran into them. They were burned and so was he. He died from the burns, but not right away."

When I told her about how Johnnie had been seen spinning a bottle, she laughed knowingly. It fit the description of the little bundle of energy she was connecting with. "He's still running around those halls," she told me.

I hope the baby with the battered face can soon let go of the calamity of this plain and move toward love and light. If you visit the St. James, enjoy the adventure, but before you leave say a prayer for Johnnie—and the other little spirits Nancy says reside there.

Chapter Three

SCHOOL SPIRITS

School is out and everyone has left. But the empty corridors echo with the distinctive thump of footsteps. Somewhere a locker slams shut. A chair scrapes across the floor. Eerie, childlike laughter floats from a vacant classroom, and the custodian nervously hurries to finish mopping the floors.

No, this is not the opening scene of an episode of *The X-Files*. This is a familiar scenario on hundreds of campuses across the country. Janitors, students, secretaries, and teachers are among the many witnesses of ghostly activity at schools.

As parapsychologists will attest, old buildings where tragedies have occurred are prone to hauntings. Schools are often witness to generation upon generation of pupils moving through their halls. Wherever there are people, there is death—sometimes sudden death. And wherever there is death, there may be ghosts not ready to move on. The following stories are testimony to that.

River of Death

In the far northwest corner of Georgia, the little town of Chickamauga is tucked in wooded foothills. The streets are wide and clean
and lined with gnarled oak trees. Most of the homes are old and lovingly cared for. Attending church is an important and regular part of
a Chickamauga family's routine in the close-knit community.

Cove Road slices through the center of town, winding its way
to the heart of Chickamauga, Gordon-Lee Memorial High School.
A sweeping lawn with graceful willow trees and sturdy oaks leads up
to the proud brick school with its stately white-columned front
porch.

Inside, artist Don Troiani's paintings of somber-faced generals
line the main hall. They seem to peer at you, their eyes following as
you hurry past.

Students here are serious scholars. In fact, 92 percent are university bound, according to Greg Greenhaw, the school's former history
teacher and athletic coach. But that is not the only distinction that
makes Gordon-Lee Memorial special. "The school is haunted,"
insists Coach Greenhaw. From 1992 to 1995 he spent his days on the
lovely campus. When night melted over the town and darkened the
hallways of the high school, *no one* wanted to be there.

"It was an eerie feeling to be there at night," said Coach Greenhaw, who was often called by local police when something was
amiss. "I was the only teacher who lived in town," he explained. So
when a light suddenly, inexplicably, came on in a second-floor classroom, or when a routine check found a door mysteriously unlocked,
officers would call Coach Greenhaw. They told him they needed a
school employee along, out of protocol. But the coach would tease

them. "You guys are afraid of ghosts," he'd say, yawning as he accompanied them through the creaking halls.

Most of the time, the police would just smile and admit nothing. But one elderly officer confessed the truth. "He told me he heard laughter and voices when the school was empty," said Coach Greenhaw. The senior officer also heard the frequently reported phantom footsteps marching down the hall and was kept busy checking out lights that winked on without reason.

Who haunts the old school? Constructed in 1932, the building was originally a boarding school. Over the years, students and teachers have naturally passed away. But Greg Greenhaw pointed to a more likely cause of the haunting. "In 1862, the Battle of Chickamauga was fought less than two miles from town," he explained. "Twenty-five thousand people were killed in two days."

The town itself was the union headquarters. A stately home was turned into the hospital for the endlessly injured soldiers. (It still stands today as the Gordon-Lee Mansion Bed and Breakfast!)

On nearby trails, a sharpshooter rode his horse, aiming his rifle at the enemy, whom he was able to spy even at night with the aid of colored glasses. When a return bullet finally blew him off his horse, the dead man was not stopped. To this day, night hikers report being confronted by a pair of glowing eyes. They've nicknamed the phantom Green Eyes.

Gordon-Lee students are familiar with the tale of Green Eyes, yet many dismiss it as nothing more than fireflies combined with overactive imaginations. But there are those, like Coach Greenhaw, who remain open-minded.

They do, after all, spend their days in a haunted school. They've *felt* General Robert E. Lee's portrait staring at them. And they've heard the inexplicable marching in the empty halls. There is no dismissing the macabre name of their cozy little town. Once called, Crawfish Springs, after American history's second bloodiest battle, it was renamed Chickamauga.

As Greg Greenhaw explained, "That means River of Death."

Dinah's Last Dance

Neither students nor professors enjoy being alone in the Boise State University communication building. Perhaps if they were *really* alone they would not mind. But when the ghost of a disturbed student joins them, the chills on the back of their necks make it hard to concentrate.

Legend says the lonely spirit belongs to a young girl who once had stars in her eyes as she waited for the boy she adored to pick her up for a school dance. But when he did not show up, Dinah went to the dance alone. She saw her love in another's arms and fled in tears. She went back to her dorm and hanged herself.

Today, that dorm is the Idaho school's communication building. Witnesses report drafts from nowhere, phantom footsteps, and lights that turn themselves on.

In Boise, the ghost of Dinah spies on those who work late in the communications building.

A Dozen Haunted Campuses

1. University of Washington, Seattle

The campus hangout, the College Inn Pub, is haunted by the ghost of a man who was murdered while visiting the campus decades ago. A frightened waitress recently heard his gravelly voice call out, "Ten feet beyond the wall! Ten feet beyond the wall!"

2. Green Mountain College, Poultney, Vermont

Students and security guards here insist that the apparition of a dwarf appears at the foot of the bed when couples are intimate. The legend of the lonely ghost says he worked at the school and died of an illness in the attic where he lived.

3. University of Minnesota, Minneapolis

Students and security guards have witnessed odd things on the Minneapolis campus. Mysterious howling has been heard in the Walter Library, and a guard claims an unseen presence threw a phone book at him in Nicholson Hall. According to lore, Pioneer Hall is haunted by a dorm official who was murdered by a religious cult.

4. Yale University, New Haven, Connecticut

Phantom music has been heard by a half a dozen witnesses as they stood beside the old organ in Woolsey Hall. In addition to the ghostly organist, Professor Harry Jepson is believed to haunt the hall that he had refused to set foot in while he was alive.

5. Vassar College, Poughkeepsie, New York

The house advisor's apartment in the east wing of Jewett House is reported to have a closet that is home to a gentleman ghost who wears a Panama suit. Children shouting and laughing are often heard in another room of the same apartment. A resident there claimed he was alone in the shower when he felt something brush his leg. Occupants believe the place is haunted by an advisor. The campuses and main building and library are also thought to be haunted—the last by a deceased librarian who is seen on the stairs.

6. Berry Junior High School, Lebanon, Ohio

Students at this school whisper about the Ghost of the Stairway to Nowhere. Her apparition is often seen near the mysterious staircase. They tell the tale of a girl who hanged herself at the top of the stairs when her boyfriend dumped her. Others insist the ghost belongs to a former female English teacher.

7. University of North Carolina, Chapel Hill

Legend says that in the early 1800s, two students here both fell for the same girl. Agreeing to let a gun decide who would win her hand, they met for a duel on a sylvan hill near the Chapel Hill campus. The loser, Peter Dromgoole, took a bullet in the chest and keeled over on a big, flat rock. The witnesses buried Peter beside the rock.

Confused over the disappearance of her love, the girl spent hours sobbing on the rock, unaware he was buried there. Sixty years later, the surviving boys confessed to what had happened. The bloodstained rock was eventually moved to a spooky stone building that students insist is haunted. The rock remains today.

8. University of California, Berkeley
In the 1960s, a troubled student tried to end his suffering by leaping from the school's Sather Tower. But the act did not stop his torment, as his ghost is said to stalk the ground around the tower, sometimes chasing female students.

9. University of the South, Sewanee, Tennessee
Students here claim to see a horrifying headless apparition at several campus locations. The ghost is seen in a gown and believed to be a student who once wore the traditional gown of the Order of the Gownsmen. Decapitated in a car accident, the young man's head is said to materialize during finals week.

10. South Eugene High School, Eugene, Oregon
The auditorium of this school is haunted by a boy who died there in 1957. He was crossing a catwalk when he stumbled to his fate onto the seats below. An eerie, cold sensation washes over those who sit where the boy died. Inexplicable sounds emanate from the area and some report seeing a ghostly blue light. A brick once dropped from overhead, narrowly missing a student beside the haunted seat.

11. University of Nebraska, Lincoln
Two ghosts are believed to haunt the Lincoln campus. Lucy was a free-spirited hippie whose short life came to a sad end

when she jumped from the fifth floor of her dorm. Her waiflike specter has been seen in nearby Pound Hall where books inexplicably pop from shelves. The other ghost is a student who was studying acting in the 1940s, spending his days rehearsing for a part in *Macbeth,* when he climbed the overhead rigging, slipped, and crashed to the stage. Witnesses report spying his ghost near the stage whenever *Macbeth* is performed.

12. University of Missouri, Kansas City

The school of architecture is believed to be haunted by the ghost of a girl who died after a botched abortion. Students report flickering lights and mysterious shadows in the empty hallways.

The University of Missouri, Kansas City campus, is home to restless spirits.

Chapter Four

PARANORMAL
PETS

They love us unconditionally. They forgive our bad breath, sloppy manners, and poor judgment. They are there nuzzling us with their cold noses when we need them most. We are comforted by their wonderful, mysterious purring and warm silky fur or by their wildly wagging tails as they greet us. They are our loyal four-footed friends.

Sadly, our animals' life spans do not match ours. The heartbreak of good-bye is part of loving a pet. Though death may take them, it is not always a *final* good-bye. For the creatures who loved us in life often continue to do so from beyond.

When I was nine years old, we had a houseful of pets. Toby, our collie-shepherd mix went out roaming one day and returned carrying a paper bag. When we peered inside to see what Toby had brought us, a tiny kitten peeked out. We named him Gogo.

The Séance

Louisa Swann was just ten years old when she attended her first and last séance.

The Nevada writer recalled the sunny afternoon when she joined several younger neighborhood children in their backyard playhouse. "Our dog Blackie had just died," Louisa remembered. The regal border collie mix had been a faithful member of her family for sixteen years. Emulating the séances they had seen on television, the youngsters lit candles in the dark clubhouse and joined hands. Louisa spoke in a hushed voice. "Blackie, are you here?"

The others tried not to giggle as the silence stretched out. Louisa tried again. "Blackie, if you are here, speak to us now."

Nobody laughed *this* time, for Louisa was answered with a loud, "Woof!" It was beloved Blackie's distinctive deep bark. "We all took off running," Lousia said, with a laugh.

Gogo, a black fluffy cat with a sweet nature, soon became a favorite. When he was about five years old he passed away. The night of the day he died on the veterinarian's operating table, my mother was awakened by a thunderous purring. In the dark, she could not see the kitty and assumed it was one of our two surviving cats. She got up for a glass of water and opened the door to my room on her way back to bed. There, sound asleep on *my* bed, were our two cats.

She concluded that Gogo's ghost had come to say good-bye.

Our family is not the only who was visited by departed pets. I've met many people with similar experiences, some which I'd like to share here.

A Loyal Friend

Bookkeeper Betty Moerer and her daughter Briana will never forget the day fifteen years ago when they first saw the little ball of fluff they named Muffy. The affectionate puppy immediately wiggled her way into the Moerer family's hearts. An Australian cattle dog, Muffy grew into a beautiful creature with shimmering red fur, accented by a white-tipped tail, a white star on her forehead, and an adorable white nose.

She soon became keeper of the family's Renton, Washington, home, tagging after seven-year-old Briana and patrolling the yard. "She looked after all of us," Betty remembered.

A sensitive soul, Muffy was attuned to her family. "She always knew when we were coming home!" Betty told me. No matter what their schedule, Muffy would go to the window five minutes before a family member's arrival, her ears perked and her tail wagging with excitement. Muffy's sixth sense was never wrong. Soon after her enthusiastic display, a loved one would always arrive.

The years passed, and as Briana grew up, Muffy grew old. The dog enjoyed thirteen years of love from her family before she succumbed to kidney failure.

Betty was heartbroken. "She and I had a special bond," she confided. Soon after she lost Muffy, Betty had a reassuring dream. Muffy appeared and led her on a long walk to a serene lake. The dog leapt into the water, yet the lake remained calm. "There was not so much as a ripple. I knew it was a sign that she was okay." The dog tossed her head, motioning for Betty to follow. But her mistress awoke.

Was the dream a spirit visit from Muffy? Perhaps so, for Betty's loyal friend has apparently not yet left her. Sometimes an inexplicable rush of air will swish by, and in the same instant Betty's heart fills with such warmth that she could swear her beloved Muffy was beside her.

And then there are the curious actions of the family's other pets. Sophie and Chelsea, the Moerers' new canine kids, often appear to be playing with an invisible dog. They sometimes leap up, alert eyes following something across the room. Then they begin chasing the presence, happily frolicking with a pal only they can see.

Yet at times both Betty and Briana *have* seen Muffy! "Usually I just glimpse her back end as she's walking around the pond," Betty told me. At other times she's spotted Muffy's full image, standing beside the roses. She kept quiet about these sightings until Briana admitted that she too had seen their deceased pet.

As she fingered Muffy's worn metal tags, which she likes to keep near her, Betty confessed, "I feel as if she is still looking after us." A sighting of Muffy serves as a warning that something is not right. "It makes me stop and pay attention to my environment."

It seems her loyal friend is still looking after her.

The Cranbury Cat

The Cranbury Inn in Cranbury, New Jersey, is made up of several very old structures, including two eighteenth-century colonial taverns and a rustic nineteenth-century post-and-beam barn. The taverns were built at a stagecoach stop for weary travelers to refresh themselves.

Today the inn is a popular restaurant that serves up such specialties as salmon en croute and ostrich carpachio *and*—some insist—ghosts!

Sharon Hecker told me about the night she and a group of coworkers celebrated Christmas together at the Cranbury Inn. As they dined, she and a friend, Joanne Crandall, who had heard of the ghost sightings, regaled the others with the tales. "Some people have seen the ghosts of a cat and a dog," Sharon told her friends.

When Joanne and Sharon got up to head for the ladies' room, they were joined by Roseanne Pudlak. "I've never seen a ghost," complained Roseanne, as they entered the rest room. "I would love to see one."

While she ducked into a stall, Joanne and Sharon were chatting by the sink when they were startled by an apparition dashing by. "It was the back end of a cat," Joanne told me.

"We saw its back legs and tail," added Sharon. "And then it disappeared."

Roseanne exited the stall too late to see the ghostly cat. "I *always* miss the good stuff!" she cried.

As the three left the rest room, they were startled by a sudden noise. "All three of us heard a resounding *meow!*" confided Sharon. "To say we were startled is an understatement."

Cranbury Inn owners Tom and Gay Ingegneri make no secret about the ghosts. "We have five people ghosts and a ghost cat and a ghost dog," Gay told me. "The cat has been seen by a bartender and many of my customers."

She often feels the cat brush past her ankles and has caught glimpses of it from the corner of her eye. She prefers to keep the description of the ghosts to herself, as a way to authenticate the many sightings.

Six Places to See Ghostly Animals

1. Clifton, Arizona

For over a century now, startled people have encountered Fantasma Colorado (Spanish for Red Ghost) near Chase Creek. The apparition of a huge orange camel with a corpse tied to its hump is thought to be a remnant from a U.S. Army expedition in 1857.

2. Pet Cemetery, Los Angeles, California

The spirit of Kabar, Rudolph Valentino's Great Dane is said to haunt his grave site. Some report that they can hear the panting of the ghost dog, who died in 1929. Others swear that the big dog has licked their hands.

3. Mentone, Alabama

Locals have long reported seeing the apparitions of Granny Dollar and her faithful dog, Buster, roaming the woods near the spot where her cabin once stood. The disgruntled ghost was believed to be restless because the money she saved for her tombstone was stolen when she died in 1931. In 1973, she finally received her stone and has not been seen since. But Buster, who was put to sleep when she died, is still seen trotting through the forest.

4. Newberry, South Carolina

Folks who walk along Old Buncombe Road sometimes get the shock of their lives when a big white dog suddenly leaps out at them. The Hound of Goshen is believed to have patrolled a five-mile ribbon of the road since the 1800s. Those who venture between the church cemetery and Goshen Hill may see the ghostly hound pass right through wrought-iron fences to pursue them. Most witnesses are running too fast to get a good look.

5. Casper, Wyoming
The magnificent image of a galloping white stallion has been seen in Rattlesnake Range. While alive, he was nicknamed White Devil by ranchers, because of his reputation for attacking those who tried to lasso his friends, the free-spirited wild mustangs. White Devil still patrols the area, his ghostly form cutting a brilliant image against the stark backdrop.

6. Port Tobacco, Maryland
A bloodstained boulder called Peddler's Rock is said to be home to Blue Dog. Locals say that two centuries ago a peddler was robbed and killed here. Blue Dog guards his dead master's buried gold. Blue Dog's apparition and his eerie howling are most often witnessed in February.

Abby and Noble

Then there are the cases of pets and their humans who return together, such as in the haunting of Hotel Vendome in Prescott, Arizona.

Hotel Vendome is a charming two-story brick building with a wide, inviting front porch. It is located in a historic neighborhood and surrounded by lovely Victorian homes. A visit to this classic hotel is like taking a step back in time. Its twenty-one rooms feature beautiful antiques and claw-footed tubs that are original to the 1917 structure.

Those strolling by may catch a glimpse of the ghosts of Abby Byr or her cat, Noble, peeking out from behind the lace curtains of Room 16. Mr. and Mrs. Byr owned and lived in the hotel in the early 1900s. The couple lost the hotel because of unpaid taxes. But the new owners kindly allowed them and their cat to stay. Mr. Byr eventually moved on, but Abby and Noble stayed and stayed. Many insist they are *still* there.

Owner Kathie Langford is not sure she believes in ghosts. "But you won't catch me sleeping in Room 16!" she told me.

Room 16, it is said, is the room where the kitty and her mistress passed away. Guests report that both the heater and the television turn themselves off. The latter seemed to be making a statement when reporters stayed in the room.

"They were watching an episode of *Sightings,*" Kathie said. As the group sat engrossed in the TV program, featuring hauntings, the image suddenly winked off. The TV appeared to be dead.

"They couldn't get it to work again until the show was over," said Kathie.

Guests and employees alike have spotted the apparitions of both Abby and Noble.

Rama Patal, the hotel's previous owner, said that in her six years overseeing the Vendome, "No one was ever afraid. Abby and Noble are happy spirits."

His Master's House

Ruth Anne and Bob Boender bought a turn-of-the-century Tudor house in Seattle, Washington, in the early 1990s. Damaged in an arson fire a few years before, it had been partially restored, and the Boenders set out to finish the renovation.

The house was full of charming features, such as an open window in the wall between the kitchen and the dining room—a shortcut for serving meals.

As one winter night crept into morning, Bob was at the house working late. He was determined to make progress putting in a new kitchen floor. As he knelt below the pass through window, he had an odd sensation. "It felt like something was dripping on my head," he said.

Puzzled, he glanced up. There, poking out of the opening, was a German shepherd's head. "He was snarling and growling," said Bob.

Terrified, Bob rushed from the house.

He stood outside in the frigid air. How could a dog have gotten into the house? And it was no ordinary dog, for in order for the animal to look through the opening, he would have had to have been *floating* several feet in the air. Bob had seen a ghost.

He got his courage up and returned the next day. The couple managed to finish the remodel and soon made the house their home.

"After we moved in, we often sensed a presence," Ruth Anne confided. She and Bob and their two sons frequently saw a little brown dog at the edge of their peripheral vision. Whenever they spun around for a better look, the image vanished.

They didn't really mind the presence of the animal spirits. The little dog was harmless, and the frightening German shepherd never made another appearance. But it was a little unsettling the day an intruder got into the house.

Bob was in the dining room when he spotted the stranger in his kitchen. It was a disheveled middle-aged man. He wore a rumpled suit and a goofy grin as he waved at Bob. He looked like a nut. How had he gotten in?

Bob hurried to confront the stranger, but suddenly the fellow was *outside* the locked door, still smiling and waving at him through the window. When Bob went outside to talk to him, he was gone.

Shortly after, an acquaintance stopped by with an article about the previous owner. Bob took one look at the accompanying photo and shouted, "That's him! That's the man who was in my kitchen!"

His friend shook his head. "That's impossible," he told Bob. "He's been dead for several years."

As the story unraveled, the Boenders learned that the man had lived in their house during the arson attack. A gangster wanna-be, he had made enemies who apparently wanted him dead.

He escaped the fire and moved to another place, where he soon died under suspicious circumstances. Some suspect he was murdered.

Curious to learn more, Bob struck up a conversation with a neighbor, who revealed a sad detail about the arson. "Two dogs died in the fire," she told him.

"Was one of them a German shepherd?" asked Bob.

"Why yes!" the surprised woman replied. "It was a beautiful German shepherd named Smoke. And there was a little brown cock-apoo called Cocoa."

Now it made sense. The angry dog who had lunged at Bob was simply protecting his master's house. *Smoke.* It was a prophetic name for a beast who would perish in a fire.

Did the master come back to calm Smoke when he realized the Boenders meant no harm—that they were, in fact, saving the burnt-out house?

He certainly had appeared pleased as he smiled and waved at Bob. Perhaps he was saying, Thanks for saving the house! I came to get my dogs and we're leaving now. Good-bye.

It was, after all, the last time they were ever seen.

Chapter Five

GHOST TRILOGY

W hitefish, Montana, in the northwest corner of the state, is a favorite destination of travelers. Twice daily an Amtrak train chugs into town, blowing its mournful whistle as it approaches the picturesque city. Rimmed with majestic blue mountains, downtown Whitefish exudes an old-fashioned charm. Historic, lovingly cared for brick buildings line the wide, clean streets. Children under eighteen scurry home before the 10 P.M. curfew horn blares its warning, a long, low note that sets every dog in town to howling.

It seems such an innocent place. Yet, Whitefish has its secrets *and* its ghosts. I've chosen three whose lives (and deaths) intersect where visitors embark, lovers embrace, and strangers watch the city flash by from train windows: the railroad station.

The Writing on the Wall

Joey Meyers unlocked the front door of the Remington and flicked on the light inside the combination restaurant, bar, and casino where she worked as manager. She glanced around, her brown eyes traveling over the still slot machines and into the quiet bar beyond. Something was wrong.

"Hello?" she called. "Is anyone here?"

No one answered. It was 11 A.M., and she was opening the business for the day. The historic building should be empty.

She shrugged off the uneasy feeling and proceeded through the casino, past the restaurant, and toward the bar. Everything seemed as it should be. The chairs were perched on the tables and the floor was mopped clean. Sparkling wineglasses hung from their places above the long oak bar. Then she saw it: a cigarette burning in an ashtray. Closer inspection revealed bright red lipstick marks at the base.

Joey quickly searched the area but found no one. She was rattled but not completely shocked. It was not the first odd occurrence at the Remington.

A section of the Amtrak station houses a historical society, run by enthusiastic volunteers and packed with information. "I'm writing a book about ghosts and researching the Remington," I explained to one of the historians there. "I understand it was once a hotel. Hauntings can often be traced to a suicide or murder. Has anything like that ever happened there?"

The historian's face turned an angry red. "A book about *ghosts?*" he demanded. "Oh, I wish you wouldn't write about the Remington. It's not haunted."

"Do you believe in ghosts?" I asked.

"No!" he barked. "I've lived here my entire life and have never heard rumors of ghosts until recently. It's all a bunch of baloney. It's stories like this that make my work as a researcher difficult."

"I want to be accurate," I persisted. "That's why I'm here."

He shook his head and said sternly, "There has *never* been a murder or a suicide at the Remington." I will save the man the embarrassment of naming him, for I soon proved him wrong. At the nearby office of the hometown newspaper, the *Whitefish Pilot*, I repeated my question.

"I have no way of knowing," the receptionist replied. "Nothing is cataloged or on microfilm." She waved her arm toward the back of the long rectangular room. "We have most of the old newspapers and you're welcome to look through them, but they aren't in any kind of order. I doubt you'll find what you're looking for."

Heavy stacks of dust-laden books held thousands of original copies of the *Whitefish Pilot,* dating back to the turn of the century. I ran my fingers over their spines and felt the hairs rise on the back of my neck as I neared the 1920s. I pulled out a book and lugged it up onto a counter. The old papers were cracked and yellowed, the corners crumbling as I turned the pages. Yet they were intact and complete, even to the old advertisements and comics.

Within minutes of random searching, I laid my hands on several tragic accounts that seemed somehow significant. I made photocopies and went on my way. I had no idea that I had found not one but *three* key pieces of the puzzle.

Smack in the middle of downtown Whitefish, at 130 Central Avenue, the Remington is airy and meticulously kept. Employees are friendly—and a little bit jumpy. For besides the living, breathing beings that walk among them is something else.

"We call him George," Joey said. "Whenever something odd happens, we joke that George did it." She recalled the afternoon a coffeepot levitated off the burner and dropped to the floor.

Then there was the time the kitchen clock flew off the wall. "It hung from a hook and there was no way for it to fall by itself," said chef Sean Thompson, who witnessed the phenomenon. "The clock had to be lifted up before it could come down.

"But weird things happen here all the time," he added, pointing to the rack above the stove. "The spoons jump off the rack. And a couple of times I've heard a man call my name when no one else was here."

"George likes to tease me by pulling on my apron strings," confided waitress Elaine LaBonte. "He's taken my car keys several times."

It seems the Remington presence has a fascination with keys. Joey shivered, remembering

Chef Sean Thompson has seen spoons leap from their hooks in the Remington kitchen.

when her spare set of master keys disappeared. "I kept them hidden in my office," she explained. "One day I went to get them and they were gone."

A few months later, people with fond memories of the old days stopped by and asked for a tour. "We hadn't opened for the day yet," said Joey. "We were the only ones here. As I showed them around upstairs, we heard a tremendous pounding on the walls. It sounded like hammering. The visitors assumed we were remodeling.

"One of the ladies noticed a dresser she remembered. The drawers had been lined with beautiful flowered paper, and she asked to see if it was still there." The dresser, in a room piled with furniture, was facing the wall. Joey and the visitor dragged it out and turned it around. "We opened a drawer, and there were my missing keys."

The woman had happy childhood memories of playing at the hotel when it was run by the kindhearted proprietor, Mokaturo Hori. Joey couldn't help but wonder if Mr. Hori was saying hello.

In 1908, Mr. Hori purchased the building on a stump-infested street and turned it into Hori's Café and Hotel. At the time, the area had a reputation as a red light district. But Mr. Hori's place was heralded as a "respectable establishment," often catering to high-class guests. In fact, President Teddy Roosevelt stayed there.

Hori's Café featured fresh vegetables from his garden. The most expensive food on the 1915 menu included T-bone steak and crab salad for fifty cents each. But there was always a pot of aromatic soup on the stove for those with no money.

The Hori family lived above the restaurant, where, after years of prosperity, Mokaturo died of stomach cancer in November 1931. Some believe he haunts the Remington, but the apparitions don't resemble him, so Joey began blaming weird happenings on "George." She thought she'd plucked the name from the air, but I suspected Joey was more psychic than she realized.

"Joey," I began, "have you ever heard of the Radium Hotel?"

She shook her head.

"That's what this place used to be. Hori's Café was on this level, and the Radium was upstairs."

Her eyes grew large as I handed her a copy of an article from the *Whitefish Pilot* for November 14, 1919. The headline dominated the front page: BRAKEMAN GEORGE WINANS KILLS SELF IN HIS ROOM. WELL KNOWN RAILROAD MAN IN DESPONDENCY OVER ILL HEALTH LOCKS HIMSELF IN ROOM AND SEVERS HIS THROAT WITH RAZOR.

George Winans, a brakeman out of Whitefish, took his own life sometime between Wednesday morning and Thursday afternoon, in his room at the Radium Hotel. He came in from a run the last of the week and seemed to be in his usual spirits. He visited with friends, however, on Saturday evening, and they remarked to him that he did not seem like himself, but he passed it off as a joke. . . .

[O]n Thursday the suspicion of the hotel management was aroused after repeated alarms at the door of his room, and the door was found locked on the inside. By calling help and looking over the transom, the body was seen on the bed with the throat cut and a razor in the dead man's hand. . . .

The article stated that George had been working out of Whitefish for three years and was well liked and that the morgue was waiting for instructions from his parents, who lived in Two Rivers, Washington. It described how he had stopped by the newspaper office a week earlier to say he was going to Spokane for an examination and thought he would be able to go back to work. The paper went on to say, *It is assumed that worry over ill health was the cause of his rash act.*

Joey and I hurried up the wide carpeted stairs to search for the fateful room. The front section of the hotel had been turned into management offices, but a back hallway and a half dozen of the original hotel rooms were still intact.

BRAKEMAN GEORGE WINANS KILLS SELF IN HIS ROOM

Well Known Railroad Man in Despondency Over Ill Health Locks Himself in Room and Severs His Throat With Razor.

George Winans, a brakeman out of Whitefish, took his own life some time between Wednesday morning and Thursday afternoon, in his room at the Radium hotel. He came in from a run the last of the week and seemed to be in his usual spirits. He visited with friends, however, on Saturday evening, and they remarked to him that he did not seem like himself, but he passed it off as a joke. Fellow workmen say that he has been acting somewhat melancholy and depressed of late.

The callboy called him about 4 a. m. Wednesday to go out on a run but received the reply that he did not want to go out if they could find anyone else. Later in the afternoon he was called again but no response was received and it was assumed that he was not in the room. Finally on Thursday the suspicion of the hotel management was aroused after repeated alarms at the door of his room, and the door was locked on the inside. By calling help and looking over the transom, the body was seen on the bed with the throat cut and a razor in the dead man's hand. The coroner was notified and the body was removed to the Waggener morgue and relatives notified.

Winans had been working out of Whitefish for the last three years, but had not worked much the last month or so on account of health. In the Pilot office a little more than a week ago he said he was going to Spokane for an examination and thought he would be able to go back to his work. He was well known around town and was a most likeable young man. It is assumed that worry over ill health, with the possibility of a permanent break down of health was the cause of his rash act. His friends and acquaintances are very much grieved by his untimely death. His parents live at Two Rivers, Wash., and no additional action will be taken till they are heard from.

"That's the waitresses' dressing room." Joey pointed to a door and grinned. "But they won't change in there. They say it feels like someone is watching them."

Most of the rooms were used for storage, several stacked with old furniture. "I wonder which room he was in," I mused out loud. I was struck by a thought so powerful it was nearly a voice. *I didn't kill myself. I was murdered. Please tell my parents. Tell my sister! Tell Sarah!*

"He could have been murdered," I ventured. We looked out the window at the rooftop of the adjacent building. It was just six feet or so lower than the room we stood in. "It would have been easy for the killer to escape," I observed.

My gut said that a young man fearing for his health wouldn't kill himself in a lonely hotel room. He would go home where his mother could feed him soup and plump up his pillows.

Remington manager Joey Meyer laughs in amazement at the discovery of significant writing on the basement wall.

The Hotel Radium in the early 1900s, where George Winans drew his last breath.

Was it suicide or murder? Whichever, I felt sad for George.

No numbers marked the doors, but we tried to assign them in case we could learn which room George had died in. It was a frustrating task, because the rooms in the front part of the hotel no longer existed. It was impossible to guess where the sequence started.

"Let's go to the basement," I suggested.

Cavernous and gray, the basement stretched the length of the building, with a hodgepodge of mysterious rooms and stairways to nowhere. Decades before it had housed the bar. Small cubicles, now just cobweb covered shells, had long ago served as apartments for many of Whitefish's Japanese immigrants.

Today the basement is used for storing such things as wine and holiday decorations. It took some coaxing but Joey came with me, trailed by several employees who had been caught up in the excitement of the investigation. Armed with a flashlight, Joey trained the beam on the walls as we read the old writing—mostly carpenters' measurements. After about five minutes something caught my eye. "Wait!" I cried, as Joey scanned the wall. "Go back!"

She moved the light back to the spot I pointed to. There, in slanting handwriting, were the words: *George #14*. In fading pencil but still distinct, the writing jumped out at us. Joey looked as if she were going to faint.

We tried, and are *still* trying, to find the original Room 14. Was this the room poor George died in? Perhaps finding the writing on the wall was just a coincidence, but what a coincidence.

Tell my parents I didn't kill myself! Tell Sarah!

Was my mind playing tricks on me? Or am I the recipient of a message from beyond? If so, who is Sarah?

Despite extensive research, I have yet to locate the town of Two Rivers, Washington, where George Winans's parents lived. Apparently it no longer exists. I did, however, find a Winans family that lived in another part of the country over a century before George. I noted with interest that both the names George and Sarah popped up frequently in that family tree. It made me wonder if the Remington's George Winans could be a descendant.

Something tells me that George's story is not yet over. I hope someday it can be tied up as neatly as the story of the second Remington Ghost.

Happy Anniversary

Joey Meyers, the manager of the Remington Restaurant, Bar, and Casino, has actually seen only one of the resident ghosts. When we sat down together in 1998 she shared the details. "It was at the employee party in mid-December last year," she said. "Everyone knew each other. It was mostly young people, employees and their families. That's why the old guy stood out."

She was chatting with a friend when she glanced up to see an elderly man in a long dark coat at the edge of the crowd. "He didn't have a drink. He just stood there, smiling and watching. I thought, *I wonder who he belongs to.*"

She glanced away for a second, and when she looked back the old gentleman was gone. His appearance had been so out of place that she grabbed the bartender and asked if she had seen him. She had not and helped Joey search for him. The two dashed outside and scanned the sidewalk, but the man had vanished.

A shiver skipped down my spine as an incredible "coincidence" occurred to me. "Your party was seventy-five years *to the month* that a man celebrated his seventy-fifth birthday here when it was Hori's Café," I said. "It was his last meal."

Joey's jaw dropped as I pushed the telltale article across the table. the *Whitefish Pilot's* December 15, 1922, headline screamed, MARK L. PROWSE STRUCK BY TRAIN, INSTANTLY KILLED.

Mark L. Prowse, a resident of Whitefish for 12 years, was struck by passenger train No. 44 at 10:28 Monday night and instantly killed. The accident happened about fifty yards from the west end of the railway bridge crossing Whitefish [R]iver, and a short distance within the yard limits. Mr. Prowse was walking along the track toward the incoming train but it is evident from a statement made by Fred Kaiding, engineer of the train, that Mr. Prowse did not see the train till it was almost upon him. He was walking along the ties outside of the rails, and Kaiding says that he was in a few feet of

Mr. Prowse before he saw him, as the train had just rounded a curve, and did not have time to sound the whistle, but had whistled at the yard limit. Mr. Prowse when he finally noticed the train, hesitated a moment and then started to turn just at the moment the train struck him. His sight was not very good and he was evidently startled when he observed the train and perhaps blinded by the bright head-light. . . .

The tragic accident happened on Mr. Prowse's seventy-fifth birthday. He had spent the afternoon and evening in town. He and his daughter, Mrs. Omnia Reynolds, had had a birthday dinner at the Hori [C]af[é], and in the evening Mr. Prowse attended the Masonic [L]odge, of which order he had been a member for more than thirty years. . . . He had been making his home for some time with his son, Garland Prowse, foreman in the Pilot *office, and was on his way home when struck by the train. . . .*

Was it possible that Mr. Prowse popped in on the seventy-fifth anniversary of his death—a death that occurred as he celebrated his seventy-fifth *birthday?* Had the festive atmosphere simulated the environment of his last day alive and somehow prompted an appearance?

If Mr. Prowse *is* haunting the Remington—*why?* What is it that has stopped the old man from moving on for nearly eight decades after his death?

"How did you find this?" Joey asked, as she studied the article.

"I'm not sure," I admitted. "It was with the other articles. It was as if someone was guiding me."

In the same way that I was drawn to the old newspaper articles, I felt drawn to the cemetery. The sun sparkled as I walked the two miles from the heart of Whitefish to the neatly kept cemetery at the

MARK L. PROWSE STRUCK BY TRAIN, INSTANTLY KILLED

Mark L. Prowse, a resident of Whitefish for 12 years, was struck by passenger train No. 44 at 10.28 Monday night and instantly killed. The accident happened about fifty yards from the west end of the railway bridge crossing Whitefish river, and a short distance within the yard limits. Mr. Prowse was walking along the track toward the incoming train but it is evident from a statement made by Fred Kaiding, engineer on the train, that Mr. Prowse did not see the train till it was almost upon him. He was walking along the ties outside of the rails, and Kaiding says that he was in a few feet of Mr. Prowse before he saw him as the train had just rounded a curve, and did not have time to sound the whistle, but had whistled at the yard limit. Mr. Prowse when he finally noticed the train, hesitated a moment and then started to turn just at the moment the train struck him. His sight was not very good and he was evidently startled when he observed the train and perhaps blinded by the bright headlight. He was struck in the right side by the pilot beam and thrown into the air and away from the track. The train was stopped at once and backed up and the body placed on a baggage car and brought to the station. Dr. Taylor, company surgeon, was notified but an examination indicated that death must have come instantly.

On Seventy-fifth Birthday.

The tragic accident happened on Mr. Prowse's seventy-fifth birthday He had spent the afternoon and evening in town. He and his daughter, Mrs. Omnia Reynolds, had had a birthday dinner at the Hori cafe and in the evening Mr. Prowse attended Masonic lodge of which order he had been a member for more than 30 years. He was a member of Whitefish Lodge No. 64, and was a past master of a Kentucky lodge before coming to Montana. He had been making his home for some time with his son, Garland Prowse, foreman in the Pilot office, and was on his way home when struck by the train Sherman & Miller took charge of the body. Funeral services will be held at 2 o'clock Saturday afternoon at the Masonic temple, in charge of Whitefish Lodge No. 64, A. F. & A M. Burial will be in Whitefish cemetery.

top of the hill. The occupants' names are listed on signs beside each row. I found Mr. Prowse almost immediately. Walking gingerly beside the graves, I saw the well-groomed stones flanking the old man's resting place. But Mr. Prowse's grave was covered with grass. Perhaps the old marker is grown over, I thought. I knelt beside it, reverently running my fingers over the cool green grass. No stone.

A thought popped into my head: *I want a headstone.*

I smiled. *That* is what he wants!

It is not something I think *I'll* care about when I die, but I understand that it is of great importance to some people, both living and dead. Many, many stories have been documented where spirits become restless when their grave markers were missing or disturbed.

Maybe one of Mark's descendants will read this and buy the poor guy a stone.

One for the Road

It is odd that the train is a pivotal point for these stories of violent deaths. George was a brakeman. Mr. Prowse was killed by a train. And a third mystery in Whitefish involved a conductor.

The Remington employees continued to regale me with their paranormal experiences—a figure seen from the corner of the eye, sudden cold drafts from nowhere, food unaccountably cooking on its own.

The image of a man in a bowler hat had been spotted at the bar.

A waitress mentioned her encounter with a vanishing man. "I was going to seat him," she said, explaining that he stood just a few feet away, facing her. "I dropped my pen and bent to pick it up. When I glanced up an instant later, he was gone."

There was not enough time for a human to disappear so completely, and she was shaken.

"Was he an old man?" I asked.

"No. He looked like he was in his thirties or forties."

Too young to be Mr. Prowse, too old to be George. The paper did not list his age, but referred to George Winans as a young man. Back in those days, you were old at forty.

Had she seen the ghost of Conductor Ben G. Ramay? He was the subject of the third article I found in the newspaper archives. He had suffered a violent death in December 1922 and might very well be a restless spirit.

But what did that have to do with the Remington? Was the Ramay home near the establishment? I could not find an address for the house that contained the long-ago tragedy. Yet the Ramay name was familiar.

I sorted through the photocopies I'd made of the *Whitefish Pilot*. Among them were several advertisements for a women's dress shop. The old-time ads were fascinating, and I'd made copies of several. The name of the store was Ramay's. Was Ramay's near the Remington?

I asked around, but no one knew—until I interviewed Emma Hennessey. A longtime resident of Whitefish, she fondly remembered shopping at Ramay's French Model Shop in the 1920s and confirmed that the shop was owned by Ben Ramay's wife. "When I was twenty I bought a red hat there," she said, with a laugh. "I thought I was gorgeous!"

"Where was the shop?" I asked.

"Right across the street from Hori's Café—where the Remington is now," she replied. Emma remembered the scandal of the Ramay murder. Her input, along with articles from the *Whitefish Pilot* archives, painted a picture of the day a family was destroyed.

December 1, 1922, was a cold Friday night when hundreds gathered in downtown Whitefish. Laughter tinkled in the air, and the sky was a starry dome. The mood was festive and filled with anticipation as they waited for the unveiling of the windows.

Eighteen shop owners had entered the contest for best window display. The grand prize was $15, and the proprietors had worked all week on their colorful displays. At 7 P.M., with lights shining behind them, the windows were unveiled. Men in bowlers grinned, ladies in fur-trimmed coats clapped their hands in delight, and children raced from window to window, exclaiming and shouting.

We can only imagine the display in Ramay's French Model Shop window. The enterprising Mrs. Ramay was proud of her classy shop and surely would have showcased her best dresses. Did she decorate the window with big paper snowflakes, or perhaps surround the entire thing with a wreath? In the end, it didn't matter, for she would lose all of her holiday joy.

Mrs. Ramay's daughter, Mary, was sweet sixteen and already married. The girl still lived with her parents, along with her seventeen-year-old husband, Raymond Douglass, a former Western Union messenger.

Hours after Whitefish citizens celebrated on Central Street, things grew ugly at the Ramay home. Christmas cheer was blurred by alcohol as tension grew between the two men of the house. That tension turned to violence as they faced off. Young Raymond wrapped his hands around a gun and aimed. With two deafening blasts, Ben fell to the floor. Blood poured from the wounds—one in his leg, the other in his abdomen.

He was rushed to the hospital in the nearby town of Kalispell and operated on at 1:30 A.M. At first his prognosis was good, but he developed pneumonia and died ten days later.

Raymond Douglass stood trial the following March. The frightened boy insisted he had shot in self-defense. He testified that his father-in-law had been on a drinking binge and was abusing family members.

For forty-eight hours, ten jurors argued his fate. Nine men were set to convict him of first degree murder. But one man held out, "Others are as much to blame as Douglass," he insisted, and persuaded the rest to agree to *second* degree murder, a verdict with a more lenient punishment. Douglass was sentenced to eighteen to fifty years in prison, with the possibility of parole in nine years.

Though stoic as he received his sentence, he broke down and wept once he was behind bars. His good name, his freedom, and his future with sweet Mary were all gone.

If Raymond Douglass served the minimum term, he was released in 1931 at age twenty-seven with enough time left to lead a full life. But Ben Ramay never kissed his wife again. Never boarded another train. Never held his grandchildren. Was he able to let go of such earthly concerns?

If Mr. Ramay *is* a ghost, is it possible that he is still hanging around a locale that played a part in his life?

Ramay's was an expensive shop where the most fashion conscious women shopped. Hori's Café was an upscale establishment where the Ramays probably dined.

Had Ben been part of the window festival that fateful Friday? Had he cheered on his wife as the windows were revealed—perhaps stopping at Hori's Café for dinner before heading home for the very last time?

If Ben *is* haunting the Remington, what does he want? Did he really abuse his family? If not, does he want his good name cleared? If he indeed was a heavy drinker, is he perhaps looking for one last whiskey?

Mark Prowse had his fatal encounter with the train just ten days after Ramay was shot. (The two men died within a day of each other.) Did these restless spirits join George in haunting the Remington? I can almost see them at the bar, slapping each other on the back, perhaps unaware of their shared predicament as they toast each other. "Just one more," Mr. Ramay might say, as he tips his glass. "One for the road!"

When I took copies of the old articles to the Stumptown Historical Society, I was excited to share the discoveries. But I encountered yet another prickly historian, a board member who had dropped by. I introduced myself to the middle-aged woman, who promptly put her nose in the air. Apparently she had heard about my paranormal research and was of the same mind as the first volunteer I had attempted to interview: *It's a bunch of baloney!*

"Would you like to see what I found?" I asked, trying to hand her the old articles.

"No!" she snapped, and stepped back as if I had offered her a tarantula.

Surprised at her rude reaction, I persisted. "You mean you won't even *read* this?"

"No!" She shook her head angrily. I shrugged and turned away. Apparently, to some, history is a subjective study.

The local historians were not the only skeptics. Waitress Charla Wright had laughed at fellow employees when they talked about the Remington's ghosts. "I was standing in the kitchen, right beside the wall underneath the knife rack," Charla told me, "when I told Joey I didn't believe in ghosts." The words had barely popped from her lips as Charla took a step forward. An instant later a huge knife shot from the rack and landed where she had been standing. "It just missed me," she said with a shudder. "Now I believe there *is* something here."

"There's *definitely* something here!" agreed John Watson, the casino cashier. Not only does he sense a presence, he has seen evidence of it. One night, when he was helping to clean up after closing time, John Watson and fellow employee John Grundy had washed the rubber bar mats and set them on the bar to dry. They left the room for a moment and returned to find a fresh dirty footprint in the middle of one of the mats. "It was from a *huge* shoe," John Watson told me. "No one around here has feet that big!"

In the end, despite all the answers revealed in the investigation of the Remington ghosts, we are still left with a bushelful of questions.

The identity of the smoking lady remains a mystery.

Perhaps no living person knows the real reason Ben Ramay died. Did his own anger and alcohol consumption contribute to his death, or was he simply a victim?

Is Mark Prowse still lingering, hoping to be remembered with a slab of stone?

"It's okay to go now," I said out loud, as I explored the historic building. "You are dead and your loved ones wait for you on the other side. Go to the light."

Did the ghosts follow my advice? Perhaps. Reports of paranormal activity at the Remington have diminished since my investigation.

If the Remington's restless spirits have more to tell us, I hope they will speak up.

Ghost Makers

Researchers believe that some deaths are more likely to result in hauntings—especially those that are so sudden and traumatic that the ghost does not realize he or she is dead. They are thought to have no sense of passing time. A century may be just seconds on the other side. Trapped souls seem to exist in a state of confusion. It may feel a little like being stuck in a dream.

Though many ghosts are thought to stay simply because they are fond of a place, most hauntings are believed to be caused by one of the following situations:

1. Murder. Unsolved killings especially seem to precipitate ghosts. Often when the murder is solved the ghost moves on.
2. Suicide. Committed in an intense state of torment, the bruised soul is in so much pain it remains earthbound.
3. Accidents. Falls, drownings, fatal fires, car wrecks, and other sudden deaths seem to be more often tied to hauntings than passings from natural causes.
4. Broken hearts. Those who die mourning a lost love or child are often traced to the source of ghost activity.
5. Greed. A preoccupation with land or money has at times been carried to the beyond. There are many reports of possessive beings who cannot seem to let go of their earthly valuables.
6. Lack of proper burial or a later desecration of the grave. Countless hauntings have been traced to missing gravestones or vandalism of a resting place.

Chapter Six

UNTIL WE
MEET AGAIN

G ood-byes can be painful. Yet, when we don't get a chance
to say them, we can be hurt even more. This must be the
reason for Farewell Spirits—my name for special "ghosts" who are
not trapped or confused. Indeed, they most likely are excited about
their new adventures in the afterlife. But they know the loved ones
they've left behind are in pain. Hence, they come to say good-bye,
to let us know they are okay.

I still can't believe that my dear friend Millie Yoacham is gone.
My mother and I met her in the mid 1980s. She was a fan of Ann's
true-crime books and began writing to her during the infamous
Diane Downs trial in Eugene, Oregon. Downs was accused of shooting her three children. Millie watched the trial and helped take notes
for Ann's book, *Small Sacrifices*.

When Ann and I attended the trial, we met Millie and fell in love with her. She was in her seventies then, but her thick auburn hair and trim figure made her appear decades younger. (When she went dancing with her granddaughter, the men they met thought they were sisters!)

My mom and I were instantly taken with Millie's wit and warmth. I'll never forget the night we spent in Millie's cozy trailer. She pampered us, and we sat up half the night talking. She also entertained us with a phone trick called Ask the Wizard. It involved her phoning "the wizard" (her daughter, Eilene Schultz), who could tell us exactly which card we'd picked from the deck. It was a convincing ruse the two had played many times on gullible friends.

Our friendship continued until (and beyond?) Millie's death a year ago. The night Millie died, my mom and I talked on the phone. We'd both had experiences with Farewell Spirits and wondered if our friend would make an appearance. "If anyone can find a way to do it, *Millie* can," said Ann.

I fell asleep, hoping it was so. After midnight, my phone rang. I stumbled out of bed and snatched up the receiver. It was hard to make sense of what the caller said. She was excited and speaking rapidly. I finally determined she had the wrong number and went back to bed. I'd no sooner fallen asleep when the phone rang again.

It was the same person. "Why are you calling me in the middle of the night?" I asked sleepily. But she kept asking *me* questions. We were getting nowhere. I went back to bed again. The phone rang again, but I pulled the pillow over my head and ignored it.

The next morning the caller phoned again. Both of us were alert now, and she explained that she had received several calls from *my* phone in the middle of the night. My number had appeared on her caller ID each time. She'd simply been calling me back because she thought *I* was waking *her* up!

"We didn't call you," I insisted. "My husband was sound asleep, and we don't have any kids."

Puzzling over the mystery, I asked her name.

"Millie."

I nearly laughed out loud! This, of course, was not *my* Millie. She sounded nothing like her. Yet I knew that Millie Yoacham had found a way to let us know she was okay. The revelation was like sunlight splashing into my heart. I told the other Millie about my friend and my theory. We chatted a little, and she told me she worked as a beautician in Seattle.

After hanging up, I phoned Millie's daughter. Eilene was as excited as I was to hear about the mysterious phone mishap. When I told her the other Millie worked as a beautician, there was a silence.

"Years ago, Mom was a beautician," she finally said.

I can't help but think of the phone game Millie played with us the night my mother and I spent in her trailer. And I smile to think she is still up to her old tricks!

I suppose skeptics could say that my friend's Farewell Spirit was not saying good-bye. They would speculate that the phone wires had somehow gotten crossed.

Yes, of course, but who crossed them?

What are the odds that another Millie would receive a call from *my* phone on that night? What are the odds that that "random" lady would not only have the same name as my friend but a shared occupation?

In my heart, I know it was no coincidence. I'd like to dedicate the following stories of Farewell Spirits to my friend Millie.

Hello Again

Tony Best of Redondo, Washington, is not one to imagine things. "I tend to be skeptical," he said, "and if anyone told *me* the story I'm about to tell you, I wouldn't believe them." But the Australian-born photographer cannot deny what his eyes so clearly saw. And after twenty years the memory is still vivid.

A joyful occasion collided with tragedy when the Best family welcomed their newborn daughter. "Stacey was two when Kimberly was born," Tony explained. "About the same time, my sister, Cynthia, became very ill."

Cynthia, thirty-four, was excited about her new niece. Unmarried and childless, she loved being an aunt. Afraid to expose her mysterious illness to the baby, she got only one quick peek at her. She couldn't wait to feel better so she could cuddle the new baby. But she stayed away and her illness grew worse.

No one knew why Cynthia died. Her family grieved, so sorry that the children would not get to know their doting aunt.

One evening, just days after losing his sister, Tony sat in the living room of his Redondo home and visited with his mother-in-law. Suddenly he heard his two-year-old daughter calling him. He went up the stairs and opened the door of Stacey's bedroom. When he flicked on the light, he saw his toddler sitting up in her bed with her hands over her face. When she pulled her hands away, Tony got the shock of his life. "It wasn't her face," he confided.

The round, chubby baby face was gone, replaced by the mature, angular face of an adult. *Cynthia!* Tony stared in wonder at his sister's face, surrounded by Stacey's fine hair. It was the exact size of little Stacey's face, but the features were Cynthia's.

The lips moved, but it was his toddler's voice that came out. "I just want to see the baby and then I'll go back to sleep." With that, the little girl got up off the bed and went down the hall to her infant sister's room.

Tony stood rooted to the spot, a wave of joy washing over him. A moment later, Stacey came back to the room. She was herself again. As Tony tucked her in, he marveled at what had occurred.

"I wasn't drinking," he insisted. He knew it was a spirit visit from his beloved sister. "It was neat that she got to come see the baby," he said, smiling at the memory.

Living for the First Time

Mandy Merrill will never forget her very first friend—though she can't remember their first meeting. Tracy and Mandy were just babies when their mothers introduced them. "She was the first friend I ever spent the night with," said Mandy, who is now a young mother. "We practically lived together for years."

Mandy adored her pal Tracy. Both pretty, popular girls from Pioneer, Louisiana, they were active in their church group and devout Christians. Mandy has sparkling brown eyes and shiny black hair, while Tracy looked like an angel with her golden hair and deep blue eyes. "She'd never cut her hair in her life," said Mandy. "It fell down her back in a corkscrew perm."

While Tracy was lovely, it was her inner beauty that made her so special. Children were drawn to her, and she looked forward to one day having a family of her own.

The pair stuck together all through school. Instilled with school spirit, they attended all the games, cheering with excitement whenever their team scored. The girls chatted on the phone constantly and were always welcome in each other's homes. "We both played ball," said Mandy. "We weren't very good at it, but we loved trying."

But when the girls reached their fifteenth year, their friendship grew strained. "I was dating a boy Tracy didn't approve of," Mandy admitted. "She must have known he was going to break my heart down the road."

At the time, Mandy had stars in her eyes and was angry when her friend criticized the boy she'd fallen for. The girls argued. The disagreement was so serious that they barely spoke for nearly a year. Finally, however, Tracy and Mandy patched things up. It seemed they had their whole lives ahead to be best friends again.

Shortly after their reunion, on a hot August day, Tracy and her mom stopped by to ask if Mandy wanted to accompany Tracy on a Church of Christ trip to Mississippi the following day.

"My mom said no," Mandy explained. "My sister was getting married in a few days and she needed my help."

The next morning, her mother woke her with grim news. Tracy had been in a car wreck on the church trip. She and a twelve-year-old boy were fatally injured.

Mandy thought her heart would break. Everywhere she looked, something reminded her of Tracy—the kitchen table where they would sit, giggling and eating cookies; the big backyard where they'd played together as children; and the angel knickknacks that seemed to be everywhere. Tracy had collected them. Sometimes Mandy spotted one in a store window that would be perfect for her friend's collection. She'd think, *Tracy would love that.* Then, with a sad shudder, she would remember. *How could Tracy be gone?*

It hurt so much to see her friend's family grieving for the special girl who would never again make them smile. It wasn't fair, Mandy thought. Tracy had been such a kind girl with so much to live for. "I loved her like a sister," she said.

Just days after Tracy died, Mandy was fast asleep in bed when she suddenly woke up. Tracy was in her room! "She was at the foot of my bed. Her features were so beautiful. She almost illuminated the room."

Mandy gazed in wonder at the angelic image of her best friend. Tracy was sitting on the end of the bed, her arm slung over a bedpost, just as she had sat so many times before.

"She never moved from the spot and would not allow me to touch her," said Mandy. Without moving her mouth, Tracy told her she was with Jesus. "She said that Heaven was beautiful. She said she was not dead but *living* for the first time."

The spirit visit brought comfort to Mandy. And though she still grieves for her friend, she knows she is in a wonderful place.

"I loved her more than anyone will ever know," she said.

Chapter Seven

ANGEL GHOSTS

Are they ghosts or are they angels? It is a question that confuses many people. What does it mean when a presence chooses not to frighten you but to help you?

Some assume it means that the spirit in question is an angel. But parapsychologists and religious leaders make a distinction between the two. An angel is widely believed to be a spiritual being who has never been human. An angel visit is accompanied by an overwhelming feeling of peace completely absent of fear. A ghost, however, is the essence of a person (or animal) who has died. What is left behind has similar qualities to that of the person who once lived. If the person was mean-spirited, the ghost is likely to be mean-spirited. If the person was kindhearted and helpful, the ghost will be the same.

Judging by the many complimentary obituaries, millions of good-hearted people have died. So it is no surprise that so many ghosts behave *like* angels! At the very least, most ghosts mean no harm. While their "help" may sometimes have the effect of frightening folks, it is probably intended to assist.

My files contain stories of everything from a ghost who straightens shoes to one who saved a beloved family pet. Here are some of my favorites.

Sick Child

Gail Saivar of San Diego, California, remembered a night long ago when she was very sick and very frightened. She was five years old and living in a huge house in St. Paul, Minnesota, that had been built in the mid-1800s.

Tears coursed down the child's chubby cheeks as she peeked through the bars of her crib at the hall outside her open bedroom door. "Mommy! Mommy!" she sobbed, until her throat was hoarse from calling.

Her mother was downstairs and did not respond to the frantic cries. Gail's head ached, and her nose was so stuffed up it was difficult to breathe. Why doesn't Mommy come? she wondered, as she eyed the hall hopefully. She could see the stairway that led to downstairs, and she watched it for a glimpse of her mother.

Suddenly, a figure appeared on the staircase. "She wore a long white nightgown," Gail remembered. The woman moved purposefully toward little Gail. "Mommy?" Gail croaked, her eyes moving up the flowing white nightgown as the figure stood over her. *"Mommy?"*

The apparition did not respond. Gail felt fright bubble up inside her. She noticed the woman had green eyes, unlike her mother's.

Then, suddenly, her fear vanished and she began to feel better. "She didn't touch me and she didn't say anything," Gail remembered. "But I felt better and was able to fall asleep."

Who was the ethereal being who came to comfort the sobbing child? Was she a deceased relative, a grandmother Gail had never met? Or was she the ghost of a woman who had lived and died in the historic home?

Though this question remains unanswered, Gail is thankful to the being who helped her fall asleep on that horrible night.

The Volunteer

Unit Eight of Denver General Hospital in Colorado is in a nondescript beige-brick building that looks like a hundred other hospital wings across the country. But nurse Sandy Maxwell knows it is unique.

Decades ago, it was the children's wing, but today it serves sick prisoners. The patients locked away here may never walk in the sun again, for this is frequently the last stop in a life of mistakes and tragedy.

Often alienated from their families and alone in the world, the patients on Unit Eight are usually very sick and hungry for compassion. Many find it from the mysterious lady who religiously makes her rounds.

"We have two nurses and two deputies on each shift," Sandy told me. "And then there is the *volunteer*."

According to Sandy, a woman deputy spotted the altruistic visitor in another building. It was late at night, and the building was supposed to be empty and locked. "Excuse me, ma'am," the deputy said politely. "No one is supposed to be in here. I'll have to ask you to leave."

The mystery woman complied. She turned and walked away—right *through* the shocked deputy!

"She was really frightened," said Sandy with a laugh. "She would not go back in that building and had to be reassigned.

"We think the ghost is Mrs. Speers," Sandy added. "She was the wife of Mayor Speers and used to volunteer here." Though Sandy has never seen her, she frequently spots the ghostly figure of a little boy. "He plays peek-a-boo with me," she said. "I see him out of the corner of my eye, but when I turn around he's gone."

Most Common Places Apparitions Are Seen

Ghosts can appear anywhere, but most sightings are reported in the following places:

1. Peering out of windows
2. On staircases
3. In hallways
4. Perched in chairs
5. In mirrors

She has also heard the notorious phantom noises that echo through the halls. The sounds seem to be left over from another time. "We hear toilets flushing and doors slamming," she admitted. All the shift's four employees have been present when this occurs. The patients are, of course, locked in their rooms.

Despite the paranormal activity she has witnessed, Sandy is still waiting for a look at Mrs. Speers. "The patients will often tell us that they see her—especially in Room 6. It is usually those who are terminally ill. I get the sense that she is there to comfort people."

Recently, two nurses were present when Mrs. Speers sat down on the bed of a startled prisoner. All three people in the room got a good look at her.

Eric, a patient in his forties, was dying of AIDS when Sandy cared for him. "He'd been abandoned by his family, and we spent a lot of time talking," she said.

One morning when Sandy brought him breakfast, Eric looked up at her with a light in his eyes and said, "There was a woman in here."

Sandy smiled. "Yes, I know about her," she said gently.

The experience seemed to change Eric. He was less frightened about death afterward.

"He found comfort in her visit, " said Sandy.

The Unit Eight building is scheduled for demolition sometime in 2002. Mrs. Speers will soon have to find another wing to visit.

Close Call

Tom Caldwell of San Diego, California, was still reeling from the loss of a beloved dog who'd been hit by a car when he rescued a stray. The terrier mix he named Charlie was a scrawny critter who'd been running with a pack of wild dogs. The little dog gladly abandoned life on the street as he snuggled into Tom's arms.

Soon after welcoming Charlie into his life, Tom took his new friend on a long car trip across country. "We stopped in St. Joseph, Missouri, so I could share a shot of Southern Comfort with Jesse

James," joked the forty-eight-year-old philosopher, explaining he poured a drink on the infamous outlaw's grave. "Charlie was loose, but I was keeping an eye on him."

Suddenly, Charlie dashed toward the busy street as Tom watched in horror. "Charlie!" he yelled, but the dog ignored him.

The groundskeeper ambled by, as the dog headed toward a speeding car, and shouted, "That mutt is going to be killed!"

Helpless, Tom winced as his pet raced into traffic. But at the last fateful instant, an invisible presence seemed to hit the animal in the face. Charlie stopped short, head snapping back with the blow. "He turned around and ran away from the street with his tail tucked underneath him," said Tom.

Who or what saved Charlie? It was Jesse James, according to Tom. "He did some terrible things in his life," he said. "Maybe he wanted to do something good."

Chapter Eight

GHOSTS AFLOAT

Deep, dark, and mysterious, it covers two-thirds of our world and hides secrets we may never discover. According to the Census Bureau, it was the fifth leading cause of accidental death in 1996. In fact, 3,488 people in the United States died because of it that year. Though it can be fatal, we can't live without it: Water.

My research has taken me to oceans, lakes, rivers, and even a *bathtub*. Dive in with me to explore cases of souls who will not—or *cannot*—vacate their watery graves.

Last Picnic

In a bustling Starbucks coffee shop in downtown Chicago, courteous *baristas* in green aprons serve lattes to throngs of businesspeople. As I sip an espresso, I ask the servers what they know about the *Eastland*.

"The *what?*" is the response. "Never heard of it."

The two people I chat with have lived in Chicago the entire twenty-something years of their lives. They are aware of Al Capone and the gangster wars that made their hometown infamous. Yet they look expressionless at the mention of one of our nation's largest maritime disasters—a tragedy that took nearly half as many lives as the *Titanic.*

"It happened just a block from here," I explain, but they have turned away to wait on customers.

Saturday, July 24, 1915, dawned as a gloomy day. But the early morning rain drizzling from the clouds could not dampen the spirits of the 9,000 folks who swarmed the banks of the Chicago River, waiting to board boats for a much-anticipated picnic.

The Western Electric Company had hired four ships to take employees and their families for a day-long cruise to Michigan City. Girls giggled and whispered to each other as they eyed the handsome young men. Mothers pushed sleeping babies in buggies, and boys raced excitedly along the shore as the ships docked beside the Clark Street Bridge.

Jack Billow, fifteen, a deckhand on the *Roosevelt,* glanced up at 7:23 as the *Eastland* was about to cast off. "My God!" he gasped. "The *Eastland* is lurching!"

Aboard the lower deck of the *Eastland,* Hubert Boettcher, twenty-one, was visiting with friends when he felt the floor tip.

"Move to the other side of the boat!" someone shouted.

The young women he'd been chatting with laughed, ignoring the command. But as cold water crept over the floor, the giggles turned to shrieks. In the next instant the ship "turned turtle," keeling over on its port side.

As the river flooded the steamer's cabin, several girls clung to Hubert. He grabbed on to a chain of people who were bobbing in the water, thrusting their faces into an air pocket. As he kicked his legs, he could feel people struggling beneath him. Hubert gallantly helped several men save panicked female passengers. They pushed them through a porthole where rescuers waited outside. Finally, Hubert climbed through the porthole, saving himself. In all, he rescued twenty but watched helplessly as many others drowned.

Meanwhile, Jack Billow, too, had joined rescue efforts, at first from a rowboat and then by leaping into the river. Despite the many heroes, there were simply too many people to save them all. The next day's edition of the *Chicago American* reported the river "thick with the bobbing heads of passengers."

"I heard the sound of five hundred women and children screaming at once," a survivor reported.

It was especially difficult for the women, who were dragged down by their heavy skirts and cumbersome shoes. Some clung to the sides of the boat, tearing off their clothing. Hundreds were trapped *inside* the cabin. Police rushed to find steel saws and electric drills to pierce the steel plates of the ship.

Meanwhile, the river was writhing with hundreds of drowning people. One woman recalled how she was forced to the muddy bottom of the river by the layers of struggling victims above her. As she sank, she was horrified at the eerie sight of baby buggies littering the river floor. With a rush of adrenaline, she managed to fight her way to the surface and survive.

Many people escaped the ship by popping out of portholes. One man, too fat to pass all the way through, refused to budge as he gulped precious air. In the death trap beneath him, victims screamed for their lives. Rescuers had no choice. They beat the man until he slid back into the ship, allowing others to escape.

Bodies were laid out in a seemingly endless row along the Clark Street Bridge. Amid the chaos, thieves took advantage of the situation and picked the pockets of the dead. An outraged mob beat up the robbers, and citizens volunteered their automobiles to carry the dead to a makeshift morgue. In the end, 835 lost their lives.

The ensuing investigation turned into months of reports of negligence on the part of the ship's captain and crew for overloading the ship and ignoring those who tried to report the problem. These men were arrested but later acquitted.

The July 1915 Chicago newspaper listed the unidentified dead only by number, as they waited for loved ones to claim them:

745—Girl, twenty years old, dark brown hair, white waist, yellow skirt, three large bone buttons on front, white gloves, black tie, white stockings, slippers

53—Woman, thirty years old, 5 feet 5 inches tall, lavender dress, lavender silk hose, black pumps

396—Boy, eight years old, 4 feet 6 inches tall, brown hair, full face, broad nose, brown suit

It took days for some of those numbers to become names. The city mourned when it learned that entire families were lost.

A picnic! What could be more festive than a picnic on a summer day? Who could have guessed that ladies in lavender who were primping in front of the mirror at six would be laid out in a morgue by nine?

Parapsychologists agree that sudden violent death confuses the soul, that those who pass in such a way are often too confounded to "go to the light." They become trapped, unaware of passing years, oblivious to changing times.

It is no wonder, then, that that long ago morgue is still swarming with ghosts. The *Eastland* passengers died before television was invented. If they *are* aware of their surroundings, they surely can't comprehend the nature of the business bustling around them. For the building where volunteers once solemnly brushed out the long hair of drowned women and sorrowfully wrapped children in blankets is now part of Harpo Studios, where Oprah Winfrey produces her TV show.

Harpo security guard Robin Hocott, who worked the overnight watch for three years, told a reporter, "I can say for sure that there are spirits walking the halls."

She first suspected something was amiss the night she got an urgent call from a producer working late in her office. "There are people outside my door!" the panicked woman cried. "I can hear them laughing!"

When Robin arrived, the woman admitted that she had opened the door to see *nothing,* yet the laughter and chatter continued. Others at the studio have reported hearing mournful sobbing, whispering, old-time music, and the marching footsteps of a large crowd.

Chicago's Clark Street Bridge where the *Eastland* capsized, killing hundreds.

Watery Graves

Five places where drowned spirits are still seen:

1. Brookdale Lodge, Brookdale, California

Built in 1923, this unique hotel has a stream running right through it. Some believe the apparition seen there drowned in the stream many decades ago. They call the girl ghost Sarah and blame her for the poltergeist-like activity there.

2. Reading, Pennsylvania

The ghosts of Mrs. Bissinger and her children, Philip, Lillie, and Molly have been spotted near Union Canal Lock 49, where she drowned herself and her offspring in August 1875 by anchoring them all with heavy rocks. The terrified children struggled to escape, but they sank into the murky water. The horrible energy from that day is said to envelop all those who venture near.

3. St. Joseph, Louisiana

For over a century, people have reported hearing the desperate screams of a dying woman in the Mississippi River. Some think she is the victim of a pirate raid upon the *Iron Mountain,* a 180-foot-long steamship that vanished in 1872 and has never been found.

4. Bellbrook, Ohio

A naive servant girl lived here in the late 1800s. Seduced by the mayor as leaves drifted from the trees, she fell in love. By the time the trees sprouted blossoms, her belly was expanding. When she presented him with the infant he coldly turned her away. The distraught woman drowned herself and her baby in Little Sugar Creek. It is said that every June her apparition can be seen beside the stream, humming an eerie lullaby.

5. Bowers Beach, Delaware

The apparition of a man who killed himself is reportedly seen here. The distraught man waded into Delaware Bay and gave his life to the salty water.

And then there is the Gray Lady. This mysterious woman has been spotted by several people, once even appearing on a security camera. Some claim that she floats rather than walks. Smartly dressed in a long gown and an old-fashioned hat, she looks as if she is indeed on her way to the picnic.

Time, they say, heals all wounds. It is an empty cliché. If you think about it, it is not really true. Those who were wounded the worst in the disaster—by hearts broken from grief—are almost all deceased. The tiniest babies to survive are now over eighty-six. Indeed, one unidentified baby boy was found alive in an air pocket of the *Eastland's* hull eight hours after the tragedy. Is he still alive? If so, he surely still carries the pain of losing his family before he could even know them. As for the other broken hearts, they were not actually mended. They simply—*eventually*—stopped beating.

Time, they should say, *forgets* all wounds! For that is what has seemed to happen, if my poll of the Starbucks *baristas* is any indication.

But if the citizens of Chicago set down their lattes and pry their eyes from their laptop computers and their cell phones from their ears, they may find the past is not really gone—especially if they take a stroll over the Clark Street Bridge on a quiet night.

Many have been startled there by bansheelike shrieks coming from the river. Luminous figures have been spotted bobbing in the black waters. Richard Crowe, a Chicago ghost hunter for over three decades, told me, "It happens so frequently that the police have become accustomed to the reports." The drowning ghosts appear so real that onlookers rush to call police, who, though now skeptical, are obliged to check them out.

They are, of course, too late.

The Great Gray Ghost

The young man thrashed about in the icy waves, swallowing mouthfuls of salt water as he desperately tried to gulp air. Just seconds earlier, the sailor had been snug aboard his British ship, the HMS *Curaçao,* with hundreds of shipmates—some of whom had become dear friends. Stunned and confused, he was unsure of what had happened. One moment, he'd been standing watch on the foredeck, and then came the explosive sound of ripping steel.

The *Curaçao* had gone down!

He grabbed a chunk of wood as it floated by and clung to it as he caught his breath. He heard shouting, swearing—and *crying.* He sensed death.

He tried not to look at the face of a corpse that bobbed in the water nearby. He did not want to know who it was. "Help!" he shouted. "Over here!" For now he remembered. The *Curaçao* had been escorting the *Queen Mary*. It was their assignment on this day in 1942 to help the crew of the magnificent ship watch out for enemy submarines.

But the *Queen Mary* was much faster than the *Curaçao*. As she performed her routine zigzag pattern, they had somehow cut into the mighty ship's path. The *Queen Mary* had sliced them in two.

"Help!" the young man called again. "Over here!"

Those aboard the *Queen Mary* and the other ships in the convoy were shocked by the accident. The *Curaçao* had split in two like a brittle branch. The screams for help were pitiful.

But rules were rules. And they had strict orders never to stop— even to save lives. To do so was to put everyone aboard in danger of attack from enemy submarines.

The *Queen Mary* charged forward, its formidable gray hulk cutting a clean path through the tumultuous waters. The crew tried not to think of the survivors left drowning in their wake.

The *Queen Mary* made her maiden transatlantic voyage in July 1936. Catering to the very wealthy, the 1,019-foot ship cut a stunning image as it traveled from Southampton to New York. The ship was so luxurious that a round-trip passenger ticket for two sold for $1,100—a small fortune at the time. And so the *Queen Mary* ruled the transatlantic seas, pampering the pampered, until World War II.

When her country called, the *Queen Mary* dropped her fancy fittings and allowed herself to be transformed into a troopship. Painted a camouflage gray, she blended in with the ocean. From a distance, she was almost invisible. This earned her the nickname "The Gray Ghost."

The mighty ship was so useful to the allied forces that Adolf Hitler demanded it be sunk. He offered a quarter-of-a-million-

dollar bonus to any submarine captain who could do so. But—
except for the hole in her bow from her collision with the *Curaçao*
—the Gray Ghost served her time unscathed. In July 1947, she
finally sailed again on a postwar voyage.

But even in times of peace, the *Queen Mary* saw tragedy. In July
1966, a boy of eighteen was crushed in a freak accident in the engine
room. Two women are believed to have drowned in the first-class
swimming pool.

It is these events, along with the tragedy of the *Curaçao* that
killed over three hundred, that many insist are responsible for the
reported hauntings aboard the *Queen Mary*. For today the sumptuous ship is permanently moored in Long Beach Harbor, California.
No longer sailing the seas, the historic vessel is a floating hotel and
museum—home to perhaps hundreds of ghosts.

Stay the night in one of the luxury cabins and you may wake, as
others have, to the sorrowful face of a teenage boy, staring at you
with large pleading eyes. Is he one of the poor sailors lost in the collision? Perhaps he thinks he can still be rescued and is looking for a
compassionate soul to help him.

And then there are the frequent sightings of poor John, the
young man killed in the engine room. "He has a beard and wears
blue coveralls," insist both the crew members and visitors who have
seen him. His lonely figure can be spotted pacing the length of Shaft
Alley, usually vanishing beside Door 13.

An entire tour group witnessed the apparition of a naval officer
near the swimming pool. Clad in navy whites, his figure was somewhat transparent as he strolled past the startled crowd.

Employees report the distinctive sound of splashing and gleeful
giggles emanating from the empty pool. Many others insist they have

seen the ghosts of women in old-fashioned bathing suits beside the water. One guard said he was there alone when someone came up behind him and pushed him in.

Perhaps most eerie of all are the pitiful shrieks heard near the area that smacked into the doomed *Curaçao*. It is as if the men left to drown all those decades ago do not know they are dead. They still scream for help.

Chapter Nine

GHOST RUSH

Once the largest city west of the Mississippi River, Idaho City owed its status to the discovery of gold in the Boise Basin in 1862. Thousands of prospectors flocked to town as entrepreneurs rushed to accommodate them. Soon more than 250 businesses thrived there, including barbershops, bakeries, pool halls, and even a bowling alley. Opera houses and theaters made their debuts there to entertain the newly wealthy.

Today, the Idaho City Chamber of Commerce characterizes the nineteenth-century hub of activity as "a bawdy, lusty town where whiskey was cheaper than water." Life was cheap too. Gunfights were commonplace, with the losers buried in the nearby Pioneer Cemetery.

When the gold was depleted, most of the prospectors left, and the once-thriving metropolis lost its luster. An 1865 fire was the first of a series that destroyed 80 percent of the town's buildings. Rich from the gold strike, the town's citizens quickly rebuilt.

Today, visitors can appreciate the sense of history in the pre-served town as they amble along the old planked boardwalks. Peer through the windows of the nineteenth-century buildings, and perhaps you will look into the eyes of the past. For according to local residents, ghosts swarm the area.

At the Merc, where an apple could once be purchased for a pinch of gold, proprietor Gerald Hillyard admitted to me that he has seen a phantom shopper walk through the store. The apparition heads to the back of the old grocery store and vanishes. And Mark Ransom, who grew up in Idaho City, confided that he too has seen a ghost.

Mark was eleven years old when he and several of his pals decided to explore Old Pioneer Cemetery. "We'd heard rumors that it was haunted," he told me, "so we decided to check it out." It was a summer night and dusk was settling as the boys trudged up the hill.

Gerald Hillyard has seen the ghost of a haunted shopper in his historical shop.

They laughed and tossed pinecones at each other as they neared the graveyard. Ambling among the towering pines, they read the names on gravestones where most of the occupants had been buried at least a century before. Other graves were grown over with weeds.

The boys wandered into the section where Idaho City's Chinese residents had been buried. "We were leaving the Chinese area of the cemetery when we saw him," said Mark. The startled boys looked up to see a foggy form glide past. "We watched it for about forty-five seconds," Mark said. "It looked like an old miner. We could see he had a short beard, and he was wearing old Western clothes—including a vest."

The startled boys stood gaping, and when they got over the shock they raced down the hill. "We ran home and told my family," said Mark, who today is a thirty-something computer technician and father of one. "Some of them admitted they had also seen ghosts there. One of my relatives said they saw the ghost of a Chinese girl standing beside a grave."

Mark's mother, Marian Ransom, revealed that Diamond Lil's, down the street, is also haunted. "I waitress there," she told me. "Odd things happen all the time."

"We do have ghosts here," confirmed owner Ric Call, who has seen apparitions appear in the bar. Built in 1862, Diamond Lil's was once the old watering hole where gold miners bellied up to the bar to whet their whistles.

Among the old-time ghosts are the spirits of the recently deceased. Ric was startled when he glanced up one day to see a friend, sitting at his usual spot. "He was the editor of the newspaper and the smartest man I ever met," said Ric. "He'd recently died from a disease."

The apparition appeared several more times. Then, one night, Ric left a rose and a shot of whiskey at the bar before closing up. "They were gone the next morning, and it was the last I saw of the ghost," said Ric.

Ghosts lurk behind the trees in Old Pioneer Cemetery.

Ghost in the Attic

According to the *Idaho Statesman*'s December 27, 1998, issue, Idaho has enacted a "Ghost in the Attic" statute. The new law dictates that neither a home's seller nor his broker is liable for not disclosing the fact a property may be "psychologically impacted."

Though a house might be the site of a suicide or homicide, the seller need not disclose the fact *unless* the purchaser puts in writing that the information is important to him. The broker must then "report the facts or specifically state to the buyer that the information will not be disclosed."

It is, of course, up to the buyer to research the property before purchase.

Chapter Ten

I'M A BELIEVER

M any of the people I interview preface their stories with, "I never believed in ghosts—until I saw one!"

Indeed, our culture does not encourage belief in the paranormal. People who admit to such experiences are often ridiculed and have learned to keep their mouths shut. Many a fascinating account goes untold because of witnesses' reluctance to share.

Thankfully, there are those who *will* speak up. It is from these credible eyewitnesses that investigators continue to learn. The following stories feature honest folks who have willingly shared their stories with me. I am grateful for their candor.

Old Lady Irvine

Marsha MacWillie is a reasonable person. The forty-something mother of five is a former forensics specialist who worked a dozen years in law enforcement. Her past career in forensics called for precise calculations. Many people may be surprised to learn that Marsha believes in ghosts. But she does—and has ever since she was fifteen years old.

It was a warm, starry night in Orange County, California, and the teenager was hanging out with her sister Kathie and her cousin Carol, who was visiting from Tennessee, and their friend Steve.

"We started talking about ghosts," said Marsha, "and someone brought up a story about Old Lady Irvine and how some kids had supposedly seen her on an old dirt road off the interstate." The Irvines were a founding family with a nearby town named for them. Apparently, Old Lady Irvine was a family matriarch.

Kathie scoffed and told the others, "There's no such thing as ghosts."

But the teens were bored so they soon piled into the car and, with sixteen-year-old Steve driving, headed out to see if they could find Old Lady Irvine. "We didn't really think we'd see her," says Marsha. "It was just something to do."

Joking and laughing, they cruised through the clear night, gray ribbons of highway gobbled up by the car as they headed out of their suburban neighborhood to a sprawling area of farmland.

The sweet night air was tinged with the scent of oranges, and stars twinkled above them. Soon the reassuring lights from farmhouses grew farther and farther apart. "That's it!" Steve said. "That's the road."

They giggled as he pulled the car onto the desolate dirt road. Suddenly a dense, low fog rolled in. "It came out of nowhere," remembered Marsha.

The car stalled. The headlights went out as Steve tried to get the car started.

And then, there she was. Old Lady Irvine drifted past the front of the car, glaring angrily at the kids. "She floated just above the fog," Marsha confided. "She glowed from within. She was holding a stick or a cane in her right hand. She wore a sheer white gown and had something white on her head."

The apparition paused as it crossed the road and stared at the kids with hatred in her eyes. There she remained for a full twenty seconds.

"My cousin is a southern Baptist, and she started praying really loud," Marsha recalled. While both Carol and Kathie buried their faces in their hands, Marsha and Steve stared back at the ghost, their mouths hanging open. Then, as quickly as she had appeared, she was gone. "Steve got the car started and we got out of there."

The Face in the Window

Jan Bergman was just six years old when she looked into the eyes of the other side. It was a warm autumn afternoon in Bellingham, Washington, in 1962. The leaves of the magnificent oak and chestnut trees were afire with fall brilliance. Long shadows stretched across the yard of a nearby home as she and two friends skipped barefoot through the tall grass. As they played beside the front porch of the old house, they sensed someone watching them.

Getting Rid of Ghosts

Parapsychologist Loyd Auerbach has an interesting method for banishing ghosts: he *annoys* them! In two decades as a paranormal researcher, he has used such devices as obnoxious music and strange light effects to chase ghosts away. It is a technique he stumbled upon by accident early in his career.

"It was a complete fluke," he said, describing the case of a Peeping Tom ghost who was bothering a mother and her teenage daughter. "He popped into their bathrooms and bedrooms. He was a ghost so he could put himself anywhere."

While Loyd was in the home investigating the case, the family's five-year-old boy was reading from a book of knock-knock jokes. "It suddenly occurred to me that it was really annoying," he said. "So we all sat around for two hours and read from the book. Every once in a while, I said to the ghost, 'This is going to happen every time you show up. We'll pester you with knock-knock jokes.' After two hours, *we* were ready to run screaming from the house. It worked. The ghost never showed up again."

Jan and her friends glanced up at the window to see a stern elderly man scrutinizing them, his eyes dark beneath his bushy brows. The children stood gaping for a long moment, their feet rooted to the ground as they stared at the man's funny hat. Jan had never seen anything like it. Tall and black, with a wide rim around it, it capped his severe face.

The man suddenly vanished, and the children raced home to tell their parents what they had seen. "Who lives in that old house?" Jan asked breathlessly.

"No one," said her mother. "The house is empty."

Today, Jan is a Des Moines, Washington, mother and bookkeeper. Though decades have passed, she vividly remembers the face in the window. "My parents later bought the house," she said. When they moved in, she was often frightened by noises in her room at night. "I'd hear someone walk past my bed," Jan said, still shivering at the memory. "I'm pretty sure I know who it was. The previous owners brought over an old photograph of the original owner. It was the man we saw, top hat and all. The old man had been dead for a long time before we saw his ghost. I guess he didn't want to leave his home."

"Longest Liver Takes All!"

Park Ranger Roby Armstrong looked up at the enormous brick fort. She stared at the image framed in one of the windows and then glanced at the two coworkers who walked beside her. "Is there anyone else on the island today?" she asked tentatively.

"Nope," came the reply. "We're the only ones here."

Not exactly.

When Roby looked at the window again, the figure was gone. She did not tell the others what she had just seen. She kept walking, trying to convince herself that she could not have seen what she knew she had.

Fort Delaware State Park on Pea Patch Island is accessible only by boat. Smack in the middle of the Delaware River, the Union fortress was built in 1859 and caged an estimated 12,000 prisoners during the Civil War. A formidable structure with its great size and iron-barred windows, it also served to protect the ports of Wilmington and Philadelphia. Today it is Fort Delaware State Park.

Throughout the warmer months, visitors can embark in boats from either New Jersey's Fort Mott State Park or Delaware's Delaware City for a journey to the historic site. Ninety acres of Pea Patch Island serve as a bird sanctuary. It is, in fact, the biggest Atlantic Coast nesting ground north of Florida for wading birds such as herons and egrets.

While the park is alive with visitors in the spring and summer, off-season it is frequented only by volunteers, park employees, and—some insist—the spirits of the dead.

Roby Armstrong never believed that Pea Patch Island was haunted. The thirty-something park ranger has spent years in law enforcement and is an admitted skeptic when it comes to the paranormal. "I had to see it to believe it," she told me.

But what she witnessed that day made little sense to her. "I saw a pirate. He was standing in the window in a beautiful green silk shirt that billowed in the wind, and he wore white silk pants."

About a year after Roby's sighting, I visited Pea Patch

Ranger Roby Armstrong once saw the ghost of a pirate, standing in a window at Fort Delaware.

Inside Fort Delaware, the spirits of Civil War soldiers are often encountered.

Island. It was in March 1999, and Roby had arranged for me to accompany her and a boatload of employees and volunteers who were making a maintenance trip to the fort.

We trudged up the long path to the fort, and as we got close Roby nudged me. "I was right about here when I saw him," she whispered. "He was standing in that window." She pointed at one of the tall, narrow windows in the upper level of the fort. "Why would I see a *pirate?*" she asked. "I didn't even believe in ghosts, but even if I wanted to see a ghost, it sure wouldn't have been a pirate! What would pirates have to do with a Civil War fort?"

I smiled. "When I was researching at the Wilmington Library, I dug into the archives and learned that this area was once swarming with pirates."

In fact, a June 11, 1933, Delaware newspaper article ventured that the city of Blackbird, approximately fifteen miles south of Pea Patch Island, was named for a notorious pirate. Old families, said the article, claimed Blackbird was a corruption of the name *Blackbeard.* The "swashbuckling pirate king" often anchored his ship, *Queen Anne's Revenge,* at nearby Blackbird Creek.

Blackbeard, also known as Edward Teach, went down on record as taking refuge in the area in 1717 after he and his "lily-livered rogues" panicked the "sedate Quaker city" of Philadelphia with a rowdy visit that prompted citizens to send word to the authorities for help.

The "giant, bull-necked man with his barbaric beard and clanking cutlass" was a frightening sight. To perpetuate his image, he braided slow-burning wicks into his hair and lit them before a raid so it appeared his head was on fire.

Blackbeard was famous both for his hidden treasure *and* for marrying fourteen women. Once asked if his wives knew the whereabouts of his treasure, he replied, "Only the devil and me know! The longest liver takes all!"

Could Roby have seen Blackbeard? Is he still roving the area, keeping an eye on his treasure? Pea Patch Island, after all, would have made a good hiding place: isolated, reachable only by boat, near his favorite territory. Maybe he *is* trying to outlive the devil so he can "take all."

Or perhaps Roby saw one of the lily-livered rogues, searching for treasure they suspect was buried there. Mean and boisterous, the colorfully clad buccaneers frightened those who lived near the water. Indeed, the plundering pirates so terrorized the shores of Delaware and New Jersey that at least one historian hints that the bad memories have been swept under the rug while "other 'nice' occurrences" are remembered and celebrated. The pirate raids are just one more chunk of history that seems to shame citizens into forgetfulness. No wonder Roby and the few Delaware historians I chatted with were not familiar with pirate raids on area shores.

Fort Delaware is swarming with the spirits of Civil War soldiers.

Want to See a Ghost?
You May Have Already Seen One!

My surveys reveal that about 14 percent of Americans are lucky enough to actually see a ghost. While skeptical curmudgeon types do sometimes see them, the sightings are most often reported by sensitive people.

Of course, many of us probably have seen ghosts and not even realized it. For instance, that pale teenage girl sitting alone on the bench in the train station or the elderly woman trudging along the side of the road may not be a living being at all. Who actually stops to check each person they encounter?

Five signs it may be a ghost:
1. The figure is unusually pale.
2. You glance away for an instant, and he or she is gone.
3. The "person" ignores you when you speak to it—though sometimes ghosts do interact with people.
4. The "person" is seen in an unusual place, such as on a deserted road or peering from the window of an abandoned house.
5. The "person" is dressed in inappropriate or outdated clothing, such as a raincoat in the middle of summer or an outfit from another era.

Roby will never forget the hollow, scooped-out feeling that accompanied her one and only ghost sighting. Her coworker, park historian Lee Jennings was more matter-of-fact about *his* sighting.

During his sixth year of working at the park, he finally spotted a ghost. "I saw a Union officer," he told me, and described the early summer evening when he guided a tour of four visitors.

As he led them around the outside of the fort, they were startled by the solid image of a uniformed officer. "We all saw him," Lee said, explaining that the apparition stood between the rest rooms and the fort, in vivid color, his arms folded. Suddenly he turned around and walked away before vanishing. "I think we saw Captain Ahl," said Lee. "I found an old photo of him, and it matches what we saw."

Employees and visitors have also had many independent sightings of a man in a black cloak; another pirate sighting perhaps? And several others reported spotting the ghost of an African-American cook in the fort's kitchen. "My wife has seen her," Lee said. "The ghost was peeking into pots."

Still others report the sound of children's laughter—when no children are present. Officers' families once lived on the island. And children *did* once run and play there as prisoners watched from the windows and longed for their own families.

It is not surprising that lost souls still linger on Pea Patch Island. Pain and suffering went along with being held captive here. At least a couple of people were shot at the fort. And prisoners of war, who often arrived in sorry shape, frequently starved to death on the premises. Between army personnel, prisoners, and pirates, Pea Patch Island is packed with persistent spirits.

For information on tours from Delaware City call (302) 834-7941.

Old News

David McGee, editor of the *Sullivan County News* since 1986, is not the least bit nervous about sharing his work space with a ghost. "We think he's friendly," he told me. The two-story brick building, erected in the 1940s, is the information hub of the small rural town of Blountville, Tennessee. While it's all business today, it was once the location of some unsavory activity. "There used to be a pool hall in the basement," David explained, adding that rumors indicate a man was shot to death there.

David, who often works late into the night, has grown accustomed to doors opening and shutting in the breezeless air and the faucet turning itself on in the men's room. "The floors creak and the lights go on and off," he admitted. "I've turned off the light in the production area, locked up for the night, and then returned the next morning to find the light back on."

Melvin Boyd, a computer technician who once worked as a printer at the *Sullivan County News,* remembered the time a former publisher tried to shoot the ghost. "He was sitting at his desk," Melvin recalled, "and he heard the front door open and then footsteps as someone approached." The terrified man shot three times at the invisible presence before him. "I helped dig the bullets out of the wall afterward," Melvin said, with a chuckle.

Another employee told Melvin that *he* saw the ghost walking down the stairs. He caught a glimpse of a gray suit, but before he could see the face the specter vanished.

Melvin, a longtime resident of Blountville, the second oldest city in Tennessee, wonders if ghosts from a Civil War battle may be responsible for the haunting. Some of the town's old houses still bear scars where cannonballs hit them.

Whatever the cause of the haunting, Melvin likes to tell how his brother-in-law used to make fun of him for believing in ghosts. "One quiet Sunday afternoon, he stopped in at the paper. Lo and behold, the front door opened and we heard footsteps walk across the floor. He turned white as a sheet and never again made fun of our ghost!"

Tea for Three

It was the middle of the night when Audrey Fortin got up and headed for the bathroom. As she passed by the kitchen, she glanced in and stopped short. "I had to look twice because I couldn't believe what I saw," confessed the Rumford, Maine, machine operator.

It was 1987, and Audrey, then in her early twenties, was living in a second-floor apartment of a big house in Portland, Maine. The old gray house with its bright red door was sliced into several comfortable units, and Audrey and her roommate loved theirs—despite the odd things that happened. The night she spotted the strange sight in the kitchen was just the beginning. Of course, in the right place and time, the scenario Audrey witnessed would be perfectly benign. But it was definitely out of place in the young woman's apartment. As Audrey stared into her kitchen, her eyes grew large. Three elderly ladies were enjoying a tea party around her table. "Two were sitting and one was standing up, pouring tea," she confided. Though the lights were out, the ghostly trio glowed, illuminating the area around them. The hostess ghost was a pudgy lady in a flowered dress, who smiled warmly at her curly-haired friends as she poured tea into dainty china cups.

Though stunned, Audrey stood for a full minute, gazing in fascination at the paranormal tea party. Without knowing why, Audrey heard herself say, "When you're done serving your friends, Myrtle, just clean up your mess."

When the ghosts did not respond, Audrey ran to tell her roommate about their surprise guests.

"She got up and went to the kitchen," said Audrey. "She saw the same thing I did." But her roommate was so shaken by the sight of ghosts in their kitchen that she ran back to bed and hid under the covers. "It really scared her," said Audrey. "She didn't like to talk about it."

The phantom tea party intrigued Audrey, however, and she quickly connected it to other odd happenings in the apartment. She called the presence *Myrtle,* because the name had tripped so easily off of her tongue.

Myrtle, it seemed, liked to borrow her clothes. Audrey would hang a favorite freshly laundered shirt in the closet only to find it mysteriously missing when she went to put it on. "The next day, it would be back," she said. "In the exact place it was supposed to be."

Whenever Audrey snuggled into bed with a copy of *Fate* magazine, a publication on the paranormal, the bed would shake violently. Was it Myrtle, excited because Audrey was reading about ghosts? Perhaps so, for the bed *always* shook when she read *Fate* but never when she chose other reading material.

And for some inexplicable reason, Myrtle was focused on a roll of shelf paper that Audrey had never gotten around to using. It sat on a table in the hall, but time after time, she would come home to find it on the floor. "At first I thought it had fallen," she explained. She began to anchor it, burying it behind other objects. Still, the roll of shelf paper managed to extricate itself from beneath the pile of things and turn up in odd places. "One day I came home and it was in the middle of the kitchen floor," said Audrey. Was the prim old lady ghost hinting that the shelves needed lining? Perhaps Myrtle was attempting to do the job herself.

Midnight Intruders

John DeLong has had the distinction of seeing three ghosts. The retired engineer encountered his first apparition when he moved into his deceased father's home in the mid-1970s. The turn-of-the-century Monroe, Washington, farmhouse had sat vacant for months after his father's death.

"My dad had mentioned that there were ghosts there," confided John. "He called them imps."

Early one morning, at about two, John got up for a snack. He flicked on the kitchen light and was startled to see a disheveled old man standing in the corner beside the wood-burning stove. Though the figure was clear, there was a thinness about the image that made it clear he was no ordinary person.

"We stared at each other for a long time," said John. "He had a salt-and-pepper mustache and beard and wore a mashed-down hat. He looked like an old drunk."

"What do you want?" John demanded.

The ghost did not respond. He edged away as John moved close.

"He had a wary expression," said John. "I think he was afraid of me."

Finally the apparition walked out of the room—right through the closed door. "It made a sound like a newspaper rattling," John explained.

In the following months, he caught sight of the ghost two other times. Both times the old man was walking through an open door.

"It was as if he were used to the layout of the house," he said. One day John shouted, "Get out of here!"

The old man did not make another appearance.

Twenty years passed before John saw his next ghost. He and his girlfriend, Linda Bjornsen, were staying in her home in the Muskrat Lake area of Washington State. Surrounded by towering pines, the house was practically in the woods. Deer and elk trails meandered through the backyard and eventually led to the wilderness.

One night, John woke from a sound sleep. "He sat bolt upright in bed," said Linda, who was yanked from sleep by the sudden movement.

John's eyes were wide and intent on something she couldn't see. Linda watched him track the invisible presence across the room.

"What is it?" she cried.

"Don't you see him?" he asked.

"See *who?*"

John explained that he had seen a Native American, wearing a loincloth and with feathers in his hair. The apparition climbed through the window and paced beside the end of the bed before exiting where it came in.

Though John had seen the figure in vivid detail, Linda had seen nothing.

A few weeks later, they were woken again. "We had a fan blowing in the window because it was a hot night," said Linda. "We awoke to a clatter as the fan was flung across the room. It wasn't as if the fan just fell over. The cord was actually stretched as if someone had tossed it."

Again, she watched John's eyes track something across the room. "It was really eerie," she said. "I knew he was seeing something."

Place Memories

A place memory is a recording of a past event that has been imprinted on the environment. Images (and sometimes sounds) are inexplicably impressed upon a place and later replayed in a phenomenon that is similar to watching a loop of movie film.

In some cases, the "ghosts" seen belong to people who are alive and well who have simply moved on and are unaware they've left a "movie" of themselves behind.

Scientists have yet to identify all the factors necessary to create a place memory. It is believed that powerful emotional events most often cause place memories to brand the environment.

Place memories are usually replayed when the conditions are right. An intense moment on a rainy July seventh night, for instance, may replay itself on another rainy night on a July seventh.

A moment later, John described what he'd witnessed. The same ghost who had made an appearance before had been in the room again. "The fan messed him up," said John, describing the bloody gashes on the man's face. "He stumbled and fell to the floor, and then *another* one came in."

The second ghost, apparently from the same tribe, stood staring at his injured friend. "Then he helped him up," said John. "He put his arm around his shoulder and helped him out through the window."

Though it seemed to John that the ghost was injured by the fan, I have not come across such a case in my research. No one can say for certain how our world affects those on the other side. And I am certainly not going to be the one to limit the possibilities of the paranormal.

But it is prudent to consider that John may have seen the reenactment of a scenario that took place in that spot perhaps a hundred years ago—long before the house was built.

Native Americans did live in that area and most certainly died there.

Chapter Eleven

HAUNTED
HOTELS

San Antonio paranormal investigator Martin Lear has a theory on why there are so many haunted hotels. He often tells those who take his ghost tour that spirits go to the places where they were most comfortable. Luxury hotels, he insists, are a favorite of ghosts who would like to be pampered in the afterlife as much as they were before death. "You don't find too many haunted Motel Sixes," he pointed out.

It is an interesting idea. Another possibility is that many such hotels are old, and with age comes history; with history comes death; and with death comes ghosts.

With that in mind, let's explore a few places where some guests checked in and never checked out.

The Geiser Grand Hotel

Baker City, in northeastern Oregon, is home to the Geiser Grand Hotel. Grand indeed, the 1889 building lives up to its name. Holding court on a downtown corner, the elegant structure begs to be stared at. The architecture is classic Italian Renaissance Revival. The corner clock tower soars to four stories, capped by a pointed roof. Inside, Viennese crystal chandeliers shimmer like diamonds in the moonlight, and mahogany columns gleam with all the splendor of the past.

Once heralded as "the finest hotel between Portland and Salt Lake City," the Geiser Grand is decidedly the most magnificent building in Baker City—and, some say, the most haunted.

Owners Dwight and Barbara Sidway pointed to the rich history of the building they saved from deterioration when they purchased it in 1996. "There was lots of living done in this hotel," said Barbara, who loves to tell the story of frontier cowboys who (to the shock of the haughty, white-gloved waiters) sometimes rode their horses inside.

Like most historic hotels, the Geiser Grand saw murder. In fact, a long-ago shooting there is said to have resulted in the first murder conviction in Baker County.

After its debut as a glamorous hotel, the building became in turn a brothel, a veterans' hospital, and a high rollers' gambling hall. In the 1940s, prostitutes reigned on the third floor. In its stint as a hospital, the building embraced fatal illness. Once the hotel changed hands when someone won it in a poker game.

Sex, sickness, and money—three prime causes of volatile situations that may ultimately result in hauntings!

The Geiser Grand became not so grand. The building was all but abandoned in 1968 and sat for twenty-five years. When the Sidways salvaged the structure, it was in sorry shape, a roofless wonder that was home to three owls, two foxes, and over a hundred pigeons.

Several years and six million dollars later, the Geiser Grand was back in all her former glory. But the Sidways had bought more than they'd bargained for. Their first inkling that something was askew came during the renovation. One day, a six-foot-four construction worker, who had scoffed at the idea of ghosts, got on the unfinished elevator. Suddenly, he discovered he was not alone. A dozen ghosts had crowded in with him. He quit on the spot, forgoing the $1,000 bonus he'd nearly earned. "That's too much for anybody to take!" he told the rest of the crew and made tracks out of there.

Though a dozen other workers resigned after seeing ghosts, the renovation was completed by the summer of 1997. One night, as the Sidways slept in Room 203, they were disturbed by rowdy guests in the room above them. "I could put my hand on the wall and feel the vibration of the music," confided Barbara. "It sounded as if there was a big party going on upstairs!"

Dwight hurried upstairs to quiet the party. He followed the laughter and music down the hall, only to have it all cut off abruptly as he approached. "There wasn't a soul up there," he said. The room was empty, the carpet clean, and the beds neatly made up.

Paranormal activity seems to be the rule rather than the exception at the Grand Geiser. Guests and employees alike have spotted the apparitions of a friendly lady in a violet 1930s-vintage dress. Another apparition appears to be that of a 1920s saloon dancer. Appearing from the waist up, she is clad in a red corset and a hat with a tall peacock feather.

The kitchen crew claims its own ghost, the Headless Chef. He is the lost soul of a poor man who was decapitated when a dumbwaiter slammed down on his head. In addition to his rare appearances, he revels in slamming doors and throwing pots and pans. Chef Bill Harp once witnessed a big carton of glassware levitate and float through the air before it crashed to the ground. "I never believed in ghosts until I started working here," he said.

Recently, a husband who usually sleeps through anything woke to a woman's sobbing. The worried man turned to his wife and gently shook her. She was sound asleep but woke up quickly. "Honey, what's wrong?" he asked. "Why are you crying?"

"I wasn't," she replied.

Sometimes guests wake to children's laughter. One couple who experienced this found potato bugs in the sink the next morning. The rooms are immaculate and there was no logical explanation for how they had gotten there. Perhaps the giggling children were playing a trick on them.

Visitors who are hoping for a paranormal adventure can ask for the Rain Room or the Train Room. The Rain Room, nicknamed for its ghostly shower, features a very clean spirit. Guests here are often startled by the sound of the shower turning on. This is followed by the distinct sound of splashing, as if someone were bathing. But when the curious investigate, the noise stops.

The Train Room is notorious for the occasional sound of a train roaring past the bed. Stunned guests called so often to report this to the front desk that the room earned a special name.

The hotel's bartenders claim there is at least one beer drinker among the ghosts, one with a craving for Budweiser. Though the bar features six beers on tap, only the Bud beer is chosen when, again and again, bartenders discover the tap open and the liquid foaming out.

The Sidways insist their ghosts are all friendly. Referring to the colorful past of the building, Barbara said, "When you've got a lot of living, you've got some dying too. What we are trying to offer is an authentic experience. If ghosts are part of it, so be it."

The Biltmore

Sumptuous. Elegant. Formidable.

These three words are the first to come to mind when describing the Biltmore Hotel in Coral Gables. This Florida hotel, a short drive from Miami, was built in 1926.

Massive columns, arching roofs, and a grand lobby all add to its beauty. The shimmering pool of clean turquoise water seems to stretch on forever. Actually, at 22,000 square feet, it *is* the largest pool in the continental United States.

In the 1930s, the pool was featured on Sunday afternoons when entertainers drew crowds of three thousand. Spectators were fascinated, watching alligator wrestling, synchronized swimming, and "boy wonder" Jackie Ott as he dove from an eighty-five-foot platform.

Rich with glamorous history, the Biltmore also saw tragedy. During World War II, the hotel was converted into the Army

Do the ghosts of murdered lovers still frolic on this Biltmore balcony?

The Biltmore was once a hospital that some patients *never* left.

Forces Regional Hospital to serve the wounded. Many windows were sealed with concrete. Government-issue linoleum covered the elegant marble floors.

The Biltmore remained a VA hospital until 1968 and was also home to the University of Miami's school of medicine. When the City of Coral Gables was given ownership of the property in 1973, the massive structure continued to sit empty until the eighties.

During this time, rumors began to spread that *something* was residing in the empty building.

The Biltmore reflected in a pond.

Locals reported mysterious lights shining through empty windows. Brave teenagers who tiptoed near on moonless nights ended up running away in fear as the sounds of eerie laughter and old-time music washed over them.

When the Biltmore reopened with all the former glory of its bygone days, it seemed to serve as a portal to the past that allowed ghosts of yesteryear to step through. A dishwasher who wandered into the country club building was startled to see the ghost of a man in a top hat, playing the piano. This was not an unusual occurrence, as hotel storyteller Linda Spitzer soon learned. She had planned to focus on historical events when she began there in 1994, but she was inundated with stories of ghosts seen by guests and employees alike.

Biltmore Reading

When Nancy Myer focused her powerful psychic ability on photographs of the Biltmore, she sounded almost shocked as she exclaimed, "There has been a lot of raunchy activity here!" She went on to say, as she studied my photograph of a Biltmore balcony, "A couple was murdered here. They were having an affair and were shot by the woman's husband." Nancy said the woman was naked—except for her jewelry.

I had spent a peaceful night sleeping in that room, but I, of course, do not have anywhere near the psychic abilities that Nancy Myers has. I was prompted to photograph the balcony only because of the way the curtains there were moved so beautifully by the breeze.

Or at least I *assumed* it was the breeze!

"A dancing couple dressed in twenties clothes has been seen in the ballroom," she said. As the spirits waltzed past the window, observers were stunned to notice they were transparent, then they vanished before the witnesses' eyes. Someone else confided in Linda that she had met a lady ghost on the thirteenth floor. The filmy apparition greeted her cheerily as she floated along, several feet above the carpet.

Dwight Sidway, who salvaged the haunted Geiser Grand Hotel in Oregon, was also involved in the renovation of the Biltmore. "The Biltmore was the most haunted site we ever worked on, bar none," he decisively stated.

He is aware of the stories of Thomas "Fats" Walsh, a gangster who ran an illicit casino on the thirteenth floor. Many believe that

Fats is responsible for the mischievous pranks played on the hotel's guests. "He pesters the guests by messing with the elevator and the lights," said Linda, who regales guests with ghost stories on Thursday nights.

Too Many Mrs. Browns

Bob Grinold does not believe in ghosts. Yet in his twenty-two years as the owner of the White House, he can't dismiss the reports of paranormal activity that swirl around his country inn, the biggest, grandest house in Wilmington, Vermont. Perched atop a hill, the sumptuous white building with its columned porch gazes out over the valley.

A mysterious hidden staircase makes a stay at this hotel an adventure. "Some of our guests spend the entire visit trying to find it," Bob told me.

Built in 1915, the White House was previously the summer home of a Mr. and Mrs. Martin Brown. Then Mr. Brown passed away, in 1964. The home was sold, and Mrs. Brown joined her husband in death a few years later. *Or did she?*

Despite his skepticism, Bob admitted that he can't help but wonder about reports that Mrs. Brown has come back to the home she loved. Doors slam by themselves. Employees often have the sense that someone is watching them. And no one can make sense of the odd fluctuations in temperature in one spot in the kitchen. "First it's hot, and then it turns cold," Bob said, shaking his head. "Then it's hot again, and then it's ice cold!"

He will never forget the morning a guest came downstairs with a strange story. She had woken in the night to see an elderly woman sitting in the rocking chair. The old lady's hair was in a bun, and she peered at the guest through wire-rimmed glasses. "I don't mind you staying here," said the apparition, "but I think *one* Mrs. Brown is quite enough!"

The puzzled guest had no inkling that a family named Brown had once owned the house. But apparently the ghostly Mrs. Brown had read the hotel register. The guest's name, too, was Mrs. Brown!

Twelve Haunted Hotels

1. John Stone's Inn, Ashland, Massachusetts
(508) 881-1778

Seven ghosts are said to haunt this old inn where Daniel Webster once gave speeches. Hidden rooms once harbored runaway slaves, including a ten-year-old girl who is still seen peering from a window in the storage room. Many have reported feeling mysterious hands close around their necks while seated in the dining room.

2. The Don CeSar Beach Resort and Spa
St. Petersburg, Florida
(800) 282-1116

The spirits of the Don CeSar builder, Thomas Rowe, and his lover, Lucinda, haunt this palatial pink hotel. Many have reported seeing the two ghosts hand in hand, reveling in a love that could not be in life. Thomas was a student in England in the 1890s when he lost his heart to a lovely Spanish lady. The two starred together in Vincent Wallace's opera *Maritana*. Lucinda's parents would not give their blessing, but the love affair continued in secret. Their special meeting place was a stone fountain. Lucinda became ill; upon her deathbed, she wrote Thomas one last love letter, vowing to meet him by their fountain. Though he married another, he never forgot his first love. He built a duplicate of their fountain at the Don CeSar. The fountain is now gone, but the lovers' apparitions are still seen on the spot.

3. Paso Robles Inn, San Luis Obispo, California (805) 238-2660

A night clerk who was killed in a fire in 1940 is believed to be responsible for phantom phone calls that originate from Room 1007. J. H. Emsley sounded the alarm that allowed everyone to escape the fire. Immediately after, the poor man suffered a fatal heart attack. Today the hotel staff is baffled by phone calls continually placed to 911 and the front desk. No logical explanation has been found.

4. Grove Park Inn, Asheville, North Carolina (828) 252-2711

The ghost of the Pink Lady has been seen wandering the huge halls of this old hotel. Clad in a party dress, the apparition has appeared and vanished in front of astonished employees. Many hotel guests—especially children—report being visited by the beautiful lady in pink.

5. Pelican Inn, Pawley's Island, South Carolina
(843) 237-2298

Many here tell of the legend of the Gray Man, an apparition of a man in fisherman's attire that often startles tourists,
who is said to warn of impending storms. His very first
appearance was followed by a ferocious storm in 1804. The
Gray Man also appeared just before the devastating hurri-
canes of 1806, 1822, 1893, 1916, 1954, 1955, and 1989.
Islanders believe he has saved thousands of lives. He is thought
to be the ghost of Percival Pawley, founder of the island.

6. Palace Hotel, Cripple Creek, Colorado
(719) 689-2992

It is believed that the ghost of Mrs. Kitty Chambers lights
candles and places them in the spots where she kept them in
life. Her ghost has been seen throughout the hotel, particularly in Room 3.

7. Le Pavillon Hotel, New Orleans, Louisiana
(800) 535-9095

Built in 1907 as the New Hotel Denechaud, this was the first
building in New Orleans to boast the luxury of elevators.
Originally owned by the Sieur de Bienville (founder of the
city), Le Pavillon is said to be home to five entities who were
discovered by a paranormal investigative team. The beings
are said to reside in various parts of the recently remodeled
pavilion. Room 930, in particular, is said to have paranormal
activity.

8. The Flanders, Ocean City, New Jersey
(609) 399-1000

Guests and staff alike have spotted the ghost of Emily as she floats through the halls here. Depicted in a large mural, the dark-haired beauty is said to be a friendly spirit.

9. Rufus Tanner House, Pine City, New York
(607) 732-0213

This remodeled turn-of-the-century farmhouse is known for its haunting by the spirit of a Civil War soldier who hanged himself in the nearby barn. His ghost has been spotted in the field behind the house.

10. The Hilton Hotel, Honolulu, Hawaii
(808) 949-4321

A beautiful ghostly woman in a blood-red dress wanders the halls here. Legend says she was murdered in the Diamond Head tower room. Some believe the spirit is Madam Peale, Queen of the Volcano.

11. Golden North Hotel, Skagway, Alaska
(907) 983-2294

Employees and guests have spotted two entities here. One is a being made of light who moves through Room 14. The other is the ghost of a young woman who died in Room 23. Many insist she is still here, waiting for her fiancé to return from a long-ago gold-mining expedition.

(Top) Who turns on the faucets at the Orcas Hotel?

(Bottom) The Orcas Hotel is home to the ghost of Octavia, who can be heard pacing the upper floor.

12. Orcas Hotel, Orcas Island, Washington

Built in 1900, this charming hotel is believed to be haunted by the ghost of Octavia, a woman who once ran the place. She has been known to turn water faucets on and is heard pacing the floor in an upstairs room.

Does Octavia's ghost still watch seagulls from the Orcas Hotel's front porch?

Octavia's spirit may be watching from the dark windows of the Orcas Hotel.

Chapter Twelve

ICE ON A
BALMY BREEZE

Key West, Florida, the southernmost tip of the United States, is a festive, tropical city that borders two bodies of water. You can literally *walk* coast to coast in minutes. From the east, the Atlantic Ocean's turquoise waters nibble at the silver-sanded shores. And from the west, warm zephyrs blow off the Gulf of Mexico, ruffling the feathers of the great gray pelicans that perch upon the weathered docks.

Famous for its key lime pie, snorkeling tours, and lively nightlife, Key West is perhaps *not* so famous for its ghosts. Yet they are there. You may sense them when the balmy breeze turns to ice as you pass Captain Tony's Saloon. Or they may present themselves as chills that skip down your spine as you tour the Wrecker's House. Better yet, you may actually see one as you glance toward the windows of Audubon House.

So many spirits seem to haunt Key West, it was difficult to decide which ones to choose. Here are some of my favorites.

The Blue Lady

Captain Tony's Saloon is *the* celebrated bar of Key West. Owned by Tony Tarracino, the colorful spot hints at past wild nights with the *hundreds* of bras strung from the ceiling. Left by female customers, the brassieres are dusty testimonials that speak louder than words.

As famous as the bar itself, Captain Tony was once mayor. One 1990 headline blared: INCREDIBLE POLITICIAN WHO KEEPS HIS PROMISES. KEY WEST MAYOR CAPTAIN TONY PLEDGED TO DRINK, GAMBLE AND CHASE WOMEN—AND HE DOES.

Performances by talented musicians draw crowds day and night at Captain Tony's. "Jimmy Buffett got his start here," Tony told me. "I gave him four beers and ten dollars for his first performance. But I didn't pay much attention because I was flirting with a blond."

While some customers are content to sip margaritas and tap their feet to the tunes, others are attracted to the poolroom, where a dead woman sleeps in the floor. Most people don't bother to walk *around* her gravestone, they walk *over* it. Embedded in the cement, the last reminder that this girl once lived reads ELVIRA EDMUNDS, DECEMBER 21, 1822. 19 YEARS OLD.

How did she get in the floor? Years ago, while building the poolroom addition on the bar, Tony found the tombstone. The area was apparently once a graveyard that was buried in mud by a long-ago hurricane. When Tony found the stone, he simply built the floor around it. Some insist that many other bodies share the poolroom with Elvira.

One rumor says that Elvira was the lover of a married mortician, and that when she became pregnant he killed her and buried her there when the building was a morgue. But this is nearly impossible to document, 179 years after the fact.

Is Elvira responsible for the disembodied voices heard echoing throughout Captain Tony's? Is she the fleeting figure seen darting in the shadows? Maybe. Or perhaps another "lady" haunts Key West's most famous bar.

Captain Tony outside his saloon, where he has seen the ghost of the Blue Lady.

It was Captain Tony who described Elvira's competition, the Blue Lady. Despite jokes about his time in office, Tony's fans insist he was an excellent mayor who worked to preserve Key West's historical significance. Indeed, his preservation efforts began in the 1960s, when he almost cut down the tree that grows in the middle of the bar. Captain Tony sat down with me in the shadow of this formidable tree. "I've never told another soul about this," he insisted.

Four decades before, he and his girlfriend, a pretty cocktail waitress, were living in an apartment above the saloon. One night after closing, they were counting the till when they glanced up to see a woman in a long blue dress in the courtyard. "That wall wasn't there back then," he explained, gesturing with his cigarette. "The bar opened into the courtyard. But the gate was locked, and there was no way for anyone to get in.

"We both saw her," Tony confided. "She glided past and then vanished. We saw her several times over the following weeks." They came to think of her as the Blue Lady. "My girlfriend was terrified," he remembered. "She was so scared she moved out."

Soon after, as Tony was preparing to enclose the courtyard, he got out his chain saw and was about to cut down the tree when an old-timer stopped him. "You can't cut down that tree," cried the elderly man. "That's the old hanging tree!"

A walking history lesson, the man described a scenario of seventy or so years before. Captain Tony's Saloon had been the combination morgue and ice-

A customer kicks her feet in glee on Elvira's grave at Captain Tony's saloon.

house. When folks wanted ice for their lemonade, they'd chip it from the bottom of the slabs of ice where corpses lay.

"We used to come here to watch the hangings," the old-timer said. He told how, as a boy, he and a friend had sat eating a sandwich as they observed the hanging of a woman. "I'll never forget it. It took a long time for her to die." He described her grotesque expression as she was slowly strangled.

The woman had been executed for killing her husband and children. The reason?

The gossip around town was that the woman had cryptically declared she'd "had a case of the ugly-wuglies."

"She wore a blue dress," the old-timer added.

The Blue Lady! Tony agreed it would not be right to cut down the old hanging tree, so he built his roof around it. Today, customers cheerfully sip drinks at a table beneath the tree, directly below the spot where a woman died in agony.

Many of those customers have to make their drinks doubles to calm their nerves when they encounter one of the bar's ghosts, according to bartender Chris Smela. "When the air is still, a cold breeze sometimes comes out of nowhere and blows through the saloon," he said. He also described inexplicable banging noises and mysteriously slamming doors.

Recently, on a very quiet afternoon, a honeymooner was alone in the ladies' room, sitting in the stall, when she heard a female voice warn, "Don't forget to jiggle the handle when you flush." She was puzzled because she had not heard the creaky rest-room door open. But she complied with the request and emerged to find the place empty. She raced out of the ladies' room, her face white as snow, and told the bartender what had happened.

The Old Hanging Tree

When psychic Nancy Myer studied a picture of Captain Tony sitting beneath the old hanging tree, she had no clues, only the shades of gray on the black-and-white photograph before her.

"Do you sense anything from the picture?" I asked.

She paused and then gasped. "Leslie!" she exclaimed. "That was a *hanging* tree!"

"Yes!" I replied excitedly. I have never gotten over the thrill of seeing Nancy hit the nail on the head.

"There was a lot of Klan activity in the area," she continued.

"That's true," I said. "I found an old newspaper article about it."

"Mostly black people were hanged from that tree," she added, explaining that they were innocent souls who were falsely accused of crimes. "They're still around," she said.

It was a difficult reading for Nancy, who did not want to be "linked" to the horrible happenings there. "There were many evil deeds around the tree," she said. "But the tree has stayed a positive energy."

I asked her about the Blue Lady. "She had very tan skin," said Nancy. "It was one of the more recent hangings. Her name was Gertrude. She was schizophrenic."

As for Elvira Edmunds, Nancy said she died in childbirth and her son later had the stone made. "She was very proper and would be quite upset if she knew she was in a bar," she said. But lucky for Elvira, she *doesn't* know, for Nancy insisted that her soul has moved on.

The regulars laughed knowingly. Many of them had either
seen the Blue Lady or knew
someone who had seen her.
Sometimes she is at the corner of
your vision. Sometimes she is
close. Sometimes she is way
across the room. But always there
is the impression of blue.

Is she stuck in those last horrible moments when she was
marched up to the hanging tree?
Or does she think it was all a
dream, the case of the ugly-
wuglies, the murder, and the
death sentence? If that is so, perhaps she is searching for her long-dead family.

**Captain Tony sits beneath the old
hanging tree in his Key West saloon.**

Many who see the Blue Lady may not even realize they are looking at a ghost. If you visit Captain Tony's and notice a woman in a
blue dress, watch her closely. She may disappear before your eyes.

I was fascinated by the account of the Blue Lady and eager to learn
more. But my search for documentation was fruitless. Many a Key
West citizen directed me to speak with a local historian I will call
Hank. "Hank knows everything!" they said. But Hank laughed when
I told him the story of the hangings. "There has *never* been a hang-
ing in Key West," he insisted.

Perhaps he would be more convincing if he had not been wrong
about the Key West lighthouse. While researching a possible haunt-

ing there, I approached Hank, who insisted that it had *never*—no buts about it—*ever* been blown down in a hurricane. Yet, *America's Lighthouses,* a meticulously researched book, noted that the Key West lighthouse was documented to do exactly what Hank said it *hadn't* in 1846. It was, according to *America's Lighthouses,* "destroyed by a hurricane that killed the keeper and his family. A sixty-foot tower immediately replaced the wrecked one."

As information repeatedly surfaces to prove historians wrong, I find myself more willing to consider word-of-mouth accounts. My gut says the old-timer who passed his tale on to Captain Tony was telling the truth.

"Robert Doesn't Live Here Anymore"

Artist House Bed and Breakfast in Key West is so named because the famed painter Gene Otto was born in the 1890 Victorian mansion and lived there with his pianist wife, Anne.

Much ado had been made over the Artist House's one-time resident, Robert the doll, who has been reported to move on his own, giggle, and peer out of windows at startled passersby. The three-foot-tall straw doll was presented to Gene at the age of five, and he promptly christened it Robert, his own first name. The child was said to blame all that went wrong on the *other* Robert, his faithful doll, who willingly took the blame.

Former owners used to try to trick each other by moving Robert around. But the joke was on them when they discovered that, though neither of them was moving him, Robert still managed to appear in different areas of the house.

The Artist House. Robert, the haunted doll, once appeared in the window here, startling passersby.

Those wishing to see Robert are advised *not* to knock on the door of the Artist House as countless curious people have done. The owners are busy, and besides, Robert doesn't live here anymore. He

(Below) Inside Artist House, Boots the cat poses below the haunted tower room where Robert the doll once made mischief.

(Right) Locals say that restless spirits lurk in the Key West Cemetery.

is now on display at the East Martello Museum in Key West, where he is caged in a glass display case.

Yet paranormal activity continues at the charming Artist House on Eaton Street. Objects have been observed leaping off of shelves, and the TV turns itself on and off.

My husband and I witnessed this when we stayed in Anne's room. Not once, but *twice,* the television turned itself off. And the channels changed on their own three other times. Thinking that perhaps a remote control in another room was the cause, we checked it out but found no logical explanation.

Perhaps the ghosts are bored now that Robert is gone and content themselves with playing with the television instead. Or maybe they just don't like what's on TV.

Friendly Ghost

Marrero's Guest Mansion on 410 Fleming Street is home to a friendly Key West ghost. New owners John Diebold, Jodie Jeck, and Heather Cochran were aware they were acquiring a ghost along with the charming bed-and-breakfast.

The prim elderly lady appears in old-fashioned clothing and has been seen floating past the front desk. She has also been spotted in the mirror, combing her hair.

"She especially seems to like Room 18," said John, who described how the ghost recently slammed a door there on a breezeless "dead-calm October" day.

Chapter Thirteen

THROUGH THE
EYES OF BABES

B abies are born with honest eyes. Pure and blue, they hold no lies. Those wide, innocent peepers can assess the world for what it is, without the limitations that our culture will eventually set for them.

For perhaps seven or so wondrous years, children may see a reality that seems to terrify many adults. Like the kid who pointed out that the emperor was stark naked, children see the truth that most grown-ups become blind to, and many of them are punished for it. If not punished, they may be ridiculed so that they stop talking about the things they see and, eventually, stop seeing them altogether.

These Three Ghosts

Shannon Gibbs can cast her memory back to a time when she saw the world through a child's eyes. "When I was six, I lived in Monterey, California," she recalled. "I had a room upstairs in the attic."

Three milky "floaty" figures shared the space with Shannon. "They were three-dimensional," she recalled, "but I don't remember their faces. It was as if they had veils."

Six-year-old Shannon thought of the ghosts as playmates and did not question the situation—though she was sometimes irritated when they woke her.

"They liked to play in front of my mirror and in my rocking chair," said Shannon. "We played with dolls and stuffed animals and had tea parties. They were taller than I was, so I always thought they were grown-ups. But now that I have a seven-year-old, I realize that anyone bigger seems like an adult to a child. It makes me wonder if my attic friends could have been the spirits of children."

One night as Shannon peacefully slept, she awoke to their urgent tugging on her blankets. "Leave me alone," she said irritably. "I don't want to play now. I'm trying to sleep."

"Get up," the ethereal voices urged. "You must get up and look down the stairs."

Finally, Sharon stumbled from bed. As she did, the floor began to shake. "The whole house was waving around. It was a big earthquake!"

She was afraid until her friends ordered, "Go to the doorway. You will be safe." She did as she was told and crouched under the doorjamb.

"When it started to subside, they told me to lie on my belly and slide down the stairs to my mom and dad's room. I made it there safely."

Ghost or Night Terror?

While experts agree that sightings by children should not be dismissed, parents should consider all possibilities. For instance, a scream in the night may signal a night terror. A night terror is an abrupt arousal from slow-wave sleep (stage three or four), most often early in the night. It is most common in young children and is frequently marked by a terrified scream. The child can appear to be awake, and may be violent, but later will usually have no recollection of the experience. Parents who suspect their children are suffering from this sleep disorder should consult a physician, as the episodes can be harmful for kids—or adults—who unknowingly put themselves in dangerous situations.

The Man with the Blue Hand

Peggy Bailey woke to a terrified shriek. A devoted mother, she leapt out of bed and rushed toward her children's bedrooms. Little Caleb sat in his bed, tears coursing down his chubby cheeks.

"What's the matter, honey?" Peggy cried, as she ran to him. She held the trembling two-year-old in her arms. "Everything is okay. Mommy's here," she soothed.

A nightmare. What else could it be? Caleb was probably upset over sleeping in a new place, she told herself. The single mom and her mother had recently moved to the rented house in Chilton, Wisconsin. Five-year-old Caitlin was excited about the adventure, but Caleb seemed frightened.

The old five-bedroom farmhouse was close to her work, and she was happy to have found it. The children each had their own rooms, with plenty of space for their toys.

Peggy had figured her little boy might be uneasy about sleeping alone for the first time, so she tried to make it as special as possible. She tucked him in with his favorite stuffed animals and told him he was a big boy with his own room now.

But night after night, the family awoke to Caleb's cries. "He began to talk about a man," confided Peggy. "He talked about the man in his room, or the man on his bed. Most often, he talked about the man with the blue hand. It got to the point where he would not even go in his own bedroom!"

Meanwhile, Caitlin was happy about the new place and cheerfully lined her dolls up on a shelf in her room. No one else seemed to sense anything—except for the Baileys' two dogs. "They frequently ran through the house, growling and barking for no reason," said Peggy. "And they refused to enter Caleb's room too."

Perdie, the smart poodle-terrier mix, was especially disturbed by the unknown presence. Peggy watched, concerned, as the little dog bared her teeth and snarled at the thin air. She had read that animals are sensitive to haunted places, and she found herself wondering if her little boy could be seeing someone from the other side, someone that the protective Perdie also sensed.

"One day my mother went upstairs to get Caleb some clothes from his room," said Peggy. "He followed her up and stood outside the door and pointed to the corner. 'Do you see him?' the child asked. His eyes were huge and frightened, pleading with his grandma to see and understand. He did the same thing with me," Peggy added, describing how the toddler would stand and point a trembling finger.

The adults could only stare at the empty corner. Was there really a man there? If so, who was he? Why was his hand blue?

Peggy did her best to listen to Caleb when he talked about the man. Even as she reassured him, she did not want to dismiss his fears. What if there *was* someone there? She did not want to make her child feel worse by alienating him. She tried to strike a fine balance between not feeding the fear and supporting her belief in Caleb.

Things got worse. Barely a night passed when the family slept without interruptions. The toddler's midnight screams became part of the routine. Peggy did her best to comfort her child, but it scared her to see him so frightened that his little body shook.

Finally, Caleb refused to enter the house when they returned from the grocery store, and Peggy knew she had to take action.

"I phoned the minister from the church I attended when I was twelve," she said. "I thought of him because he was an enormous man, six foot five. I was scared and I wanted someone big." Her minister put her in touch with another minister who lived in her area. "His name was Leon. He and a deacon from his church met with us. We went through every room of the house together and prayed that it be cleansed of the spirit. We left Caleb's room for last."

When they approached the little boy's room, Caleb stood hesitantly in the hallway and latched onto Peggy. He watched solemnly as the men prayed. Halfway through the prayer, Caleb looked up at his mom and announced, "He's gone now."

"It was slow going," Peggy confided, "but he *will* walk into the room now. I switched bedrooms with him, and he's doing fine."

Though Caleb does not want his old room back, he is a happy little boy again. Peggy is still curious about the identity of the mysterious stranger with the blue hand, but she has not researched the history of the house because, as she explained, "I'm too afraid of what I might find out."

Imaginary Friend

When the couple moved into their new home in Modesto, California, they did not inquire about its history. They knew only that the cute ranch house seemed perfect for them. And about the time they bought it, their little grandson, who often stayed with them, adopted a new "imaginary friend" he named Debi.

As the adults relaxed and enjoyed their dream house, the toddler played with his invisible buddy. The grown-ups just laughed and shook their heads. It did not occur to them that Debi was anything more than a figment of the child's imagination. And they had no idea that their dream house had turned to a *nightmare* house for someone else.

Deborah Whitlock was a vivacious woman who loved life. At thirty-two, the Modesto wife and mother worked for Sears and was slated to be their youngest female store manager. She was hardworking and dedicated to her job, but most of all she was devoted to her three-year-old daughter, C.J. It was love for her daughter that allowed her to endure the worst that any human being can—without uttering a scream. On March 25, 1988, Debi was brutally murdered in her own bed as her toddler slept in the next room.

"She was a hero," said Debi's mother, Jacque MacDonald. "If she had screamed, C.J. would have woken up. She kept quiet to save her daughter's life."

Jacque MacDonald worked tirelessly for nine years to find her daughter's killer. She campaigned to keep Debi's memory alive, plastering posters and fliers all over the city and putting her daughter's picture on pizza boxes and grocery carts. She also appeared on dozens of television programs. It eventually paid off, and the killer was caught.

As an advocate for victims, Jacque launched a thirty-minute local TV show called *Victim's Voice,* which dealt with the concerns of victims and their families. In one segment, with prior permission, she visited the crime scene where her daughter had drawn her last breath.

The house's new owners were stunned by the news of the murder but graciously allowed the video cameras inside. Jacque swallowed hard and followed the woman to the room that had been Debi's. The woman confessed to Jacque that odd things had happened there. The door repeatedly opened by itself. And when the rocking chair began to rock on its own, her young grandson had looked at her with big, solemn eyes and said, "Debi's in the chair."

Stranger still was the visit to the grocery store. When his grandmother lifted the boy to put him in the shopping cart, he pointed at the face printed on the seat and screamed, "No! I don't want to sit on Debi!" The child could not read, but he pointed to the photograph of a smiling young woman. It was one of the notices that Jacque had had placed on the cart seats. At the time, of course, the grandmother had no idea that the murder had happened in her home.

"Debi loved children," Jacque told me. It was just like her to befriend a little boy.

The Do's and Don'ts
of Getting Rid of Ghosts

by Nancy Myer

Don'ts

There are several important things that you should *not* do in a haunted environment. Do not use Ouija boards, pendulums, or tarot cards. All these implements can invite negativity further into the place. It is not wise to hold séances, either. Most people who conduct them are not well trained and do not seem to know what to do when problems arise, as they often do. Séances often make ghosts stronger and much harder to get rid of.

Excessive use of drugs and alcohol is also to be avoided. They lower your control of your mind and make the entry of negative spirits easier.

Do's

Visualize the house or location filled with dark emerald-green light. Fill the whole place with this color in your mind's eye. Then follow that with white light energy and fill the place up with that. Use strong white light like summer sunlight.

Both forms of energy are strongly positive. It is quite difficult for negative energy to stay in a place when you load it up with green and white light. While you do the visualization, pray that God will help these lost souls to release their hold on earth so they may continue their soul's journey.

You will need to repeat the visualization for several weeks. The entities have usually been around for a while. It takes time to persuade them to leave.

The Ouija Debate

Ouija comes from the French and German words for yes, *oui* and *ja*. According to some, the yes-yes board should actually be called the no-no board. Marketed as a toy by a major manufacturer, the smooth board, with letters, numbers, and YES and NO answers, comes with a triangular-shaped plastic planchette. Users ask a question while placing their fingers lightly on the planchette, which seems to move on its own to an answer, often spelling out words.

Though it's sold in toy stores, many experts insist it is *not* a game. Renowned psychic Nancy Myer cautions, "It opens a portal to the other side that is almost impossible to close." Personal experience and fine-tuned gut instinct have led her to warn against the Ouija.

Dale Kaczmarek, a paranormal investigator since 1975, echoes Nancy's concerns. In fact, on his Ghost Research Society Website, he states, "Most often the spirits who are contacted through the Ouija are those who reside on 'the lower astral plane,'" a place, some insist, where particularly disturbed spirits lurk.

Dale believes that "many violent, negative, and potentially dangerous conditions are present to those using the board."

Parapsychologist Loyd Auerbach, on the other hand, says, "The Ouija board has gotten a bad rap." He maintains that using the Ouija is simply "giving your subconscious permission to come through."

This author's advice? It's a tough call when contradictory opinions come from respected pros. Read all you can about it and make up your *own* mind.

Chapter Fourteen

NOMADIC GHOSTS

I s it possible for a ghost to follow a person? *Yes,* according to parapsychologist Loyd Auerbach. "It's up to the ghosts whether they do," he explained. "When someone dies, they can appear anywhere in the world to their friends and relatives. But usually," he emphasized, "there is a family connection."

Ghosts, according to Loyd, author of *Reincarnation, Channeling, and Possession,* are driven to destinations by their own psychology. He pointed to the case of a haunted restaurant he is investigating. "The ghosts are there because they had an association during life— plus the fact they like being around people."

In cases such as in the following story, the emotional ties between friends can also lead to nomadic behavior in spirits.

Best Friends

Gloria Kerns's* blue eyes shone as her best friend, Lauretta Lyons, posed in her new dress. "It's *beautiful!*" Gloria gasped, as she eyed the bright fuchsia gown with the glittering rhinestone buttons.

The year was 1967. The two teens, a year apart in age, had been pals since nursery school. In Burien, Washington, the girls turned heads wherever they went. Gloria was a slender, vivacious blond; Lauretta was a brunette so lovely that she was chosen to run for senior prom queen at Glacier High School.

When she stood shyly before the school assembly in the fuchsia gown, she was voted to win the honor. Gloria watched from the audience. She couldn't take her eyes off that dress! And she couldn't help but wish that *she* could wear it.

Before the year was over, she would get her wish.

Sweet-natured Gloria was always welcome at the Lyons home. She often hung out with sisters Lynn and Lauretta Lyons. She'd flop down on one of the beds in the girls' room and gossip with them about school and the kids who cruised "Pose Row," a section of street where boys showed off their hot rods. About a block from Pose Row on the corner of 152nd and First Avenue was Lou's Drive-in, another teen hangout. Gloria worked there as a carhop, serving root beer floats and twenty-five-cent hamburgers.

On Thursday, October 19, she took a break from work and ducked out the back door into the drizzly night. The air was tinged with the greasy scent of french fries as Gloria lit a cigarette and leaned against the wall, watching a fellow employee park his car on

*Name changed to protect the privacy of the victim's family.

a steep slope a few yards away. Suddenly, the brakes failed and the car jumped the embankment. Gloria had no time to react. The car ran over her.

The following Monday afternoon, as the rain continued its steady patter and the maple leaves grew soggy in the streets, seventeen-year-old Gloria was buried in her best friend's fuchsia dress.

Lauretta's voice still wobbles when she talks about it. "I was devastated," she said, handing me a photo of Gloria. The back is signed in a rounded hand: *To Lauretta, the sweetest kid I know. Stay cute! Love, Gloria.*

"The accident was a terrible shock," remembered Lauretta's mom, Clare. "I was always so fond of her."

Within a day of the tragedy, odd things began to occur at the Lyons house. "No one wanted to talk about it," confided Clare, who normally avoids the subject. "I'm a Christian and I don't like to open the door to such things." Yet she can't deny that something unusual was happening in her home—or, more specifically, in her *daughters' room,* the place where Gloria had spent so much of her time.

It began with a loud sighing. One of the girls would be alone, putting away laundry or reading, when she would hear a sharp intake of breath, followed by a long exhale. Several times, Lauretta was stunned to see a dark shadow form in the center of her room. As she watched, the misty form glided across the floor, moving purposefully until it disappeared around the corner or into the wall. "It spooked me!" Lauretta exclaimed. "But I knew it was my friend."

Then, one night, the dead girl's mother showed up at the Lyonses' door. Clare took one look at Mrs. Kerns's ashen face and knew something was wrong.

"Come in, please," she said gently. "Sit down. Can I get you a cup of coffee?"

Beacons from the Other Side: Haunted Lighthouses

There are places where you never feel alone—even when you are the only human around. It's not necessarily a good feeling. Especially when you do not know who or what is keeping you company. When the hairs on the back of your neck stand up, and you can't turn around fast enough to catch whoever tapped you on the shoulder, you may very well be at a haunted lighthouse. Ghosts inhabit lighthouses from coast to coast—including these three:

New London Lighthouse, New London, Connecticut
Built in 1909, this red brick lighthouse a mile from the east entrance of New London harbor is home to the ghost of Ernie, a lighthouse keeper who leapt to his death from the catwalk after his wife ran off with a ferry captain. According to local lore, the hapless keeper's slicker-clad ghost swabs the decks in the middle of the night, turns on the foghorn, and unties boats to set them adrift.

Presque Isle Lighthouse on Lake Huron, Michigan
More than one ghost is believed to reside at the Presque Isle lighthouse, where nonexistent lights shine in the night. According to locals, one spirit belongs to the daughter of a long-ago keeper. The other is believed to be a man named George who spent summers there. Recently, a little girl climbed the stairs to the top and came back down giggling. She claimed she'd been visiting with "the man in the tower" and later identified a portrait of him.

Point Loma Lighthouse, San Diego, California

This restored 1851 lighthouse is part of the Cabrillo National Monument on Point Loma in San Diego, California. Phantom footsteps are heard echoing on the stairs. No one has found an explanation for the eerie moaning and groaning that emanates from within the walls. Legend suggests that the ghost of Portuguese explorer Juan Rodríguez Cabrillo, who claimed the coast for Spain in 1542, is responsible for the haunting.

Point Loma Lighthouse, where ghostly footsteps are heard on the stairs.

"No thank you," Mrs. Kerns replied, her voice faltering as she spoke. "I came by to ask you about the mass schedule at your church." She explained that she needed spiritual guidance for she had been hearing her deceased daughter's sobs. The Lyonses comforted her but decided to keep quiet about their own experience with Gloria's ghost.

The phenomena at the Lyons home continued until Lauretta moved out and began a family of her own. "I know it sounds crazy," she said, shaking her head. "But Gloria *followed* me!"

When Lauretta and her first husband, Larry, settled into a rental home at 1624 135th, an invisible presence joined them. Lauretta was washing dishes when she heard a jingling and turned to see that a wire clothes hanger she had hung on a doorknob was moving. It swayed back and forth, gaining momentum until it swung completely around the doorknob.

Larry balked when his bride told him the story—until *he* witnessed the swinging hanger. The couple soon grew used to sharp raps on the window and mysterious knocking on the front door. "We had no curtains, so I didn't have to get up off the couch to see that no one was there," Lauretta recalled.

One day the couple's first baby, Regina, was sitting in her high chair with her back to the basement door as Lauretta spooned strained carrots into her mouth.

Suddenly, the distinct thump of footsteps sounded on the basement stairs. Lauretta sat frozen. The baby turned her head, watching the door as the steps grew closer. They stopped short at the top of the stairs.

Regina, grown now with a child of her own, confided, "I was always scared in that house." She shuddered as she remembered one particularly spooky night. "I was about six years old," she said, as she described how her family pulled their car into the long gravel driveway. There was no wind, yet the front door of the empty house swung open. Regina watched in horror as the door slammed shut, then opened again and again and *again* as the lights in the windows blinked on and off.

Had Gloria really followed her best friend, or had Lauretta coincidentally moved to a haunted house? The latter would seem more likely, if not for the fact that paranormal activity always increased near the anniversary of the poor girl's death.

One autumn evening when their children were little, Lauretta and Larry hired a baby-sitter and went to dinner. They returned to find police cars in the driveway as the house's lights flickered. Lauretta slapped her forehead. "Oh!" she cried. "I forgot the date." It was the third week in October, the time her friend's spirit was most active.

They went inside to find the sitter crouching in the corner, clutching a baseball bat. The terrified teenager had heard a tremendous crashing, as if furniture were being thrown about. The police answered her panicked call, searched the house, and found nothing.

"My parents had a hard time getting baby-sitters," Regina remarked wryly.

The family moved twice more, and each time the paranormal activity continued. The children's beds bucked and rocked like wild broncos, shocking them awake in the dead of night. When a shovel leapt off the garage wall and flew across the room, Lauretta was so shaken she begged her parents to help her. They rushed over and prayed with the family. That seemed to put a stop to the disturbances—for a while.

Today, Lauretta lives in a Burien turn-of-the-century home not far from where Gloria died. Also residing in the house are her teenage son, two cats, and . . . *someone* else.

Gloria? Who is to say for sure? All Lauretta knows is that she can't explain the disappearances of items from her dining room table. Vases, books, and figurines inexplicably vanish, only to reappear several days later.

Lou's Drive-in is long gone; a Taco Bell occupies the site of the tragic accident. The haunted house on 135th has been leveled and will soon be part of a new airport runway. Time marches on. But to a ghost, years may seem like seconds and decades just hours. Poor Gloria may still be stuck as the teenage girl who dreamed of wearing the fuchsia dress.

"I'll never forget Gloria," Lauretta vowed. "She was my best friend."

Judging by the continuing paranormal activity, Gloria won't forget Lauretta either.

Chapter Fifteen

SONGS FOR THE DEAD

The armonica plays such sweet music, it was once believed to awaken the dead. Invented by Benjamin Franklin in 1761, the armonica is made up of crystal bowls that spin in unison. When sensitive fingertips touch the rims, they create a vibration that coaxes pure notes to life.

In practiced hands, the armonica makes magical melodies. Famed hypnotist Dr. Franz Mesmer used one to *mesmerize* his patients. He claimed the surreal sound plunged them into deeper trances.

In the mid-1800s, superstitions ran wild. People believed the haunting music drove performers mad and evoked the spirits of the dead. In fact, the armonica was once outlawed in Germany because critics feared it was waking too many ghosts.

Farfetched? Maybe not. Many ghost sightings seem to be surrounded by music. Sometimes the specters are making music. Sometimes they seem drawn to it, as in the following story.

Final Curtain

It was 1921 in Memphis, Tennessee, when twelve-year-old Mary stood outside the place she loved most, the Orpheum Theater. A pretty girl with long curls pulled back by a white bow, she wore a crisp white pinafore and matching white Mary Janes. As a horse-drawn carriage passed, disaster struck. "Mary was either kicked by a horse or hit by the carriage," explained Orpheum volunteer Barbara Jackson, whose grandparents remembered the incident and related it to her.

In shock, the child stumbled to her feet, entered the theater, and found her seat. No one knows how much of the production little Mary got to enjoy. When the curtain fell and the lights came on, she was found dead in her seat.

"The theater burned down two years later, in 1923," said Barbara. "It was rebuilt in 1928. We must have inherited Mary, because she's still here." She's quick to point out that Mary has never disrupted a performance. "She's just a little girl," she emphasized. "And she *loved* the theater."

But Mary does do her share of mischief making. Once when a housekeeper was scrubbing an actor's marks off the stage, her cleaning supplies vanished. After a frustrating search, the supplies were found—in the commode!

Then there was the time a plumber, fixing pipes in the basement, spotted Mary leaping over machinery. "Hey!" he shouted at her. "You shouldn't be down here!" As he approached, he realized she was no ordinary child.

Barbara, who gives October ghost tours of the Orpheum, was hoping to interview him on the details, but the frightened plumber left hurriedly "and never returned."

Though Barbara has never seen Mary's apparition, she *has* felt the puzzling cold spots in the mezzanine level of the theater that often accompany paranormal activity. "It's such an odd sensation," she confided. "It feels like hot ice."

Actually, Mary is said to share the theater with six other ghosts. But she is by far the most active. Some believe it is Mary's ghost who swings on the magnificent twinkling chandeliers.

Barbara has no logical explanation for the mysterious swaying of the fifteen-foot-tall chandeliers. "They are still raised and lowered manually," she said, explaining that because the two-thousand-pound fixtures hang over the audience, a motion detector is in place to alert the staff to any impending dangerous situation. Many times the motion detectors have gone off and the dazzling chandeliers are discovered swaying in the still air.

Mary's ghost may be intrigued by the chandeliers, but it is the music she likes best. One organist insists that the little spirit is drawn to the tune of "Never Never Land."

"He says he can hear her tap dancing whenever he plays that song," Barbara told me. Once, during practice, several women stood listening as the sweet notes of "Never Never Land" filled the theater. Two of the women were stunned when they glanced toward the back of the theater and saw a ghostly girl in a white pinafore dancing, her curls bobbing as she kicked her little white shoes.

One woman felt herself drawn to the specter and reluctantly began to move toward her. "She told me she was terrified," related Barbara. "Yet she couldn't stop herself from walking toward Mary." Finally, she managed to get control of herself and hurried away from the eerie site.

What drew the woman toward the child's ghost? The image of the dancing spirit had an almost hypnotic effect. *Tap, tap, tap* went the little feet as the helpless woman headed toward her. It was almost as if they were moving to a cosmic beat, an unlikely duet of the living and the dead. Two worlds collided for an unreal moment as both felt the rhythm.

Could this same rhythm be what draws long-dead Mary to the stage? Is there a pattern in music that opens a portal to the other side? No one can say for certain, but the odd occurrences at the Orpheum certainly make one wonder.

Ebony and Ivory

Eileen Smith Betancourt has always loved antiques. Charmed by the beauty of old-time craftsmanship, she began her collection as a teenager. It is not just the object itself that attracts her but the *history* of a thing.

When she slides the palm of her hand over the worn oak of an old dining room table, she can't help but picture the families who once ate there. And when she peers at her own reflection in an ornately framed antique mirror, she imagines the faces of those who gazed into the glass before her. This is the way it is with antiques lovers. We like the stories that antiques tell. And many of us are aware that when we bring an aged object into our home, we also invite in its past and, sometimes, its *ghosts*.

When Eileen spotted the 1880s piano, she was not thinking about ghosts. "It was a beautiful old upright," said the Matawan, New Jersey, artist, "in need of repair and very out of tune."

But she sensed something special about it. Refinished, the piano glowed in cherry-wood splendor. She had the instrument repaired but ran out of funds to have it tuned. "We put it in the guest room downstairs," confided Eileen. Within days, her friend Karen, who was staying in the room, had a complaint. "She was spooked," Eileen explained. "She heard the piano playing at night."

Shortly after, Karen awoke to see a man standing in her room. "I believed her," said Eileen. Karen was not one to make things up.

A few nights later Eileen was engrossed in a book when she heard faint out-of-key notes drifting up from downstairs. "It was Chopin," said Eileen. "And it was being played badly out of tune!"

Another friend, Lori, came to visit and slept in the bedroom just down the hall from her hostess. "In the morning she told me she had seen a man at my bedroom door the night before," said Eileen.

Finally, Eileen herself got a look at her ghost. She awoke to see an elderly man peeking at her. Later, she walked into the guest room and caught him sitting at the piano. "He was an elderly but sturdy-looking gentleman in a smoking jacket," she said.

Eileen, who has always been psychic, got the impression that "He once played the piano in a men's club, where gentlemen gathered to talk, smoke cigars, drink, and enjoy male camaraderie."

He was a warm, friendly spirit and welcome in her home. But the day came when she had to move to an apartment and did not have room for the piano. "The movers were super guys," Eileen said.

"One of them fell in love with the piano." She took him aside and said, "You can have the piano—on one condition." She explained to him about the ghost. "You must promise to take good care of them," she said.

The young man broke into a wide grin and readily accepted the deal. The piano *and* the ghost went with him.

"I miss that piano," Eileen said. "It had a lot of character. I hope it and its true owner are happy and well."

Chapter Sixteen

Who Could Forget the Alamo?

I saw the Alamo for the first time in the fall of 2000. It was a sunny morning and middle-aged tourists, Instamatic cameras bouncing on fat stomachs, had turned out in droves to poke into every nook and cranny of San Antonio's pride and joy.

I kept my eyes wide open, hoping to spot the one man in the crowd who stands out—a man seen by countless witnesses. It is said that he is soaking wet, even on days when the arching blue sky is cloudless. Clad in a black cloak, he appears as real as any of the tourists who visit the Alamo. But he is not. When approached, he melts into nothingness.

To my disappointment, I did not glimpse the cloaked ghost, though I did talk to some who have. He is one of the Alamo's many apparitions.

Who could forget the Alamo? It was, of course, the sight of a bloodbath that symbolized the grit and determination of pioneers of the Lone Star State. But long before the likes of Davy Crockett and Sam Houston swaggered into town, the land belonged to others.

In the 1700s, the area we know as Texas was home to such Native Americans as the Apaches and Comanches, the latter a strong nomadic tribe who freely roamed the land on horses, living off deer, elk, rabbit, turkey, and buffalo.

The tribe ruled the land with so much grace and power the area was once known as Comanchería, literally translated from "land of the Comanche."

The Alamo hides many ghosts within its stone walls.

A cloaked ghost appears both day and night at the Alamo.

The first white settlers crept into the area around 1810, the same year that the Mexican War for Independence began. Mexico gained its independence from Spain in 1821, but the conflicts were far from over. Texan colonists, striving for independence from Mexico, clashed with Mexican troops in the following years, with the infamous showdown at the Alamo in 1836.

Built as a Catholic mission called San Antonio de Valero, the famed site was nicknamed "the Alamo" when a detachment of troops was sent from a post in Mexico named Pueblo de San Carlos del Alamo de Parras. Structured as a mission, the Alamo lacked the strategic design of a military fort. That basic flaw, coupled with the fact that the small force guarding the Alamo was not prepared for the magnitude of the attack by Santa Anna's army, doomed those who resided there that fateful February.

After nearly two weeks of warding off the Mexican army, many of those inside the Alamo were still asleep as March 6 dawned and the terrifying scream of *"¡Arriba!"* shattered the morning.

"¡Arriba!" Attack!

The Mexican army charged the walls and soon swarmed the camp, muskets firing as bodies fell limp and bloody. Gunfire gave way to face-to-face battles of swinging sabers and bayoneted muskets. It is written that even those who tried to surrender were not spared. It was a bloodbath. Most horrifying of all are the stories of the children who cowered beneath blankets in their beds. Yanked from their pathetic hiding places, they too were killed.

The ghosts of those children are thought to be among the many spirits who move within the stone walls of the Alamo. And, it seems, they remember the happier times. For it is their *laughter* that is heard ringing in the still night air.

Despite a nasty case of laryngitis that overcame me during my visit to San Antonio, I managed to cajole compelling accounts from normally close-lipped former Alamo guards I met there. Perhaps they felt sorry for me and my scratchy little voice, or maybe they were bursting to tell the stories they had kept secret for so long.

Alamo guards protect the four acres of lovely, well-maintained grounds twenty-four hours a day, seven days a week. The Daughters of the Republic of Texas, who have managed the Alamo since 1905, are nervous that stories of ghosts may overshadow the history of the place. But don't the two go hand in hand? The Daughters have discouraged guards from sharing their paranormal experiences. Though the guards I met no longer worked at the Alamo, they were at first secretive about the subject. Little by little, the stories came out.

For instance, there was the night that two guards were joking about the idea of ghosts at the Alamo. Suddenly, loud voices emanated from inside the locked building. The guards rushed inside to find the public address system turned on to a radio station, its volume all the way up.

In 1999, startled guards witnessed the apparition of a hooded monk in the courtyard on the north side of the church. The ghost walked toward a wall and disappeared through a solid spot where there had once been a doorway.

In the Cavalry Courtyard, guards have reported being caught in a herd of invisible horses. The thunderous sound of galloping hooves filled the space around them, as frantic whinnying split the air. It is as if the animals are panicking, galloping from corner to corner, trying to find a way out. This is the area where the horses were kept when the Alamo was occupied by the Texans. For thirteen days, the frightened horses were confined as gunfire filled the air.

The haunted Menger Hotel peeks over the Alamo's wall.

In the Gift Museum, voices emanate from unoccupied rooms. Many witnesses have heard a ghostly woman sobbing. Rangers frequently hear heavy pounding on the doors and phantom footsteps following them.

Unexplained noises are common in Alamo Hall, where guards have observed the furniture shaking. And many folks have reported seeing a handsome young cowboy ghost. Clad in Western boots, a duster, and a ten-gallon hat, he has been seen at least five times in recent years. A visitor who assumed he was an employee approached him to ask a question, and he vanished before her astonished eyes.

A Native American has been seen at both the Alamo and the nearby haunted Menger Hotel. Witnesses say they often hear him chanting. The Menger Hotel is just one of many San Antonio hotels believed to be haunted.

San Antonio, in fact, is one of the nation's most haunted cities— just ask Frank Sanchez. The twenty-something cook grew up there and has had more than his share of paranormal experiences, beginning with the haunting of his childhood home on Shasta Street.

"My sister and I shared a room," he told me. "We had an old man in our closet." Every night when the lights went out, the ghost followed the same routine. He left the closet, walked into the bathroom, and shut the door. Moments later, he would return and stand at the end of one of the beds. "Sometimes he'd stand by my sister's bed, and sometimes by mine."

The frightened children shivered beneath their covers. "We tried to tell our parents," said Frank. "But they didn't believe us."

Then came a memorable Christmas Eve that Mr. and Mrs. Sanchez will never forget. It was to be the last Christmas in the house, as the family was already packing for a move. After tucking the kids in, the parents were relaxing in the living room when they heard what they *thought* was their naughty children running around. They headed up the stairs to scold them and stopped short. There, right before their astonished eyes, was the ghostly old man.

"Finally, they believed us!" said Frank, with a laugh.

The family moved to a rental near Highland High School. "There was a huge stain on the kitchen floor," said Frank. "It trailed out the door and down the porch steps. My dad joked that the previous tenant must have murdered his wife and dragged her across the floor."

As the family settled into the home, they were disturbed by the sound of a dog barking in the basement. "It freaked us out because there wasn't a dog there," said Frank.

Curious about the strange phenomenon, Frank's father asked the landlord about the former tenants.

"No one's lived there for twenty-five years," he replied. "The last man to live there murdered his whole family. He shot his dog in the basement and killed his wife and children upstairs."

The mysterious stains Mr. Sanchez joked about *were* bloodstains after all.

"We moved that weekend," Frank said.

It seems there is no escaping the ghosts in San Antonio, for Frank has witnessed spirits in the apartment building of his girlfriend, Alexandra Rockwell, a San Antonio ambassador—a job that made her an official representative of the city.

The old structure on Broadway has been both a federal building and an office complex in other incarnations. Many tenants report seeing apparitions in their apartments. Frank was walking downstairs one night when he saw an old man headed down the hall. "He was wearing a heavy black coat and a bowler hat," he said. "At first I didn't think much of it. But when I went back upstairs, the man was in the exact same place, still walking."

Curious, Frank went back for another look. Again the man was still in motion but had not moved far. And there was something odd about the *way* he moved. There was no rhythm to his walk. It was as if he were gliding.

Franked glanced down. The old man had no feet! "He was floating down the hall," he said.

Alexandra confirmed that hauntings are common in San Antonio. As ambassador to the city, she knows the territory well. "Many places along the Riverwalk are haunted," she confided. "The Rocky Mountain Chocolate Factory is haunted, and so was the Bayou Restaurant."

The Riverwalk is an intriguing network of cobblestone paths, tunnels, and bridges that snake along the deep green river past numerous tempting shops and restaurants. At the Rocky Mountain Chocolate Factory, a phantom whisperer hisses employees' names and knocks bowls off the shelves.

The soon-to-be-demolished Bayou Restaurant is crawling with restless spirits. A former hostess named Julie said, "No one wanted to go into the basement. It was really creepy! Lots of people saw ghosts there," she added, explaining that the apparitions were all men thought to be killed in the nearby Alamo.

As I enjoyed breakfast in one of the many outdoor cafés on Riverwalk, I struck up a conversation about ghosts with the waiter. A troubled expression crossed his brow as he told me of the oddest thing he'd seen in the haunted city. "I was on the bus," he said. "I glanced up and saw faces pressed against the window." The four faces of the men and women were distorted against the glass from the outside.

Little Hands

Everyone in San Antonio, Texas, seems to have heard of the ghostly children of the Villa Main railroad tracks. Legend has it that a busload of kids died when their bus stalled on the tracks and was hit by a train. The names of the surrounding streets are often reported to be memorials for the dead children. It is said that those who turn off their car engines on the road beside the track are pushed over the tracks by helpful little hands.

To the chagrin of those who live in the neighborhood, thousands of people have tested this theory by sprinkling baby powder on the backs of their cars. I tried it too. The half hour I was there, a dozen other cars showed up, with ample supplies of baby powder. People smiled and waved at each other and waited patiently for their turns.

The cars *do* seem to get a push, and little hand prints appear in the powder. This writer, however, is skeptical. Research revealed that the roads were named after a housing developer's kids. No records of a bus accident have yet to be discovered.

I believe the fingerprints are there *before* the cars show up, and the powder simply lifts latent prints to the surface; the people with the most children seemed to have the most handprints! But I have to admit, it *is* difficult to explain how the cars are pushed uphill and over the tracks.

One note of caution: If you must try this experiment, be cautious; the area is said to attract a criminal element. A murder victim was found dumped here in recent years.

The young man glanced around at the other passengers, but they did not seem to notice anything odd. The apparitions remained on the window for the entire trip. "I'll never forget it," he told me.

Who were the strange apparitions who hitched a ride on the city bus, passengers who had died or victims of the Alamo?

It is just one of San Antonio's many mysteries.

Chapter Seventeen

America's
Most Haunted

A t least half a dozen sites across the country are vying for the distinction of most haunted. It is, of course, difficult to gauge levels of paranormal activity. Electronic gadgets such as electromagnetic field (EMF) detectors and thermal scanners are used by many investigators. These record EMF variations and fluctuations in ambient temperature. Science has not yet developed the definitive tool needed to ascertain data on those on the other side.

Still, it is reasonable to assume that by about 2030, the equipment used by parapsychologists today will be obsolete. For now, we must be content with crude tools and our own extrasensory perception, or ESP, a term coined by famed parapsychologist J. B. Rhine. Ghostly activity is often sporadic and subject to such conditions as the time of the year and the receptivity of the humans present. With that in mind, let's explore some of the places that are said to be America's most haunted.

The Whaley Skeleton

My investigation into the Whaley House reinforced my finding that historians often mold the past to suit their needs. For some unfathomable reason, they decide that certain deaths make for "nice, clean little stories," while others are so distasteful they must be locked away and hidden like the proverbial skeleton in the closet.

With this writing, I am releasing the Whaley House skeleton. The restless spirit of the Whaley House is a disturbed woman who seeks compassion, understanding, and—perhaps—forgiveness. Maybe when the public learns the truth, she can finally move on.

The Whaley House Museum in San Diego's Old Town is often called "The nation's most haunted house." This reputation gained momentum in 1964 when Regis Philbin and his crew investigated. As they sat in the dark, a female ghost floated into the parlor. Regis aimed his flashlight at her and she vanished.

Steve Bennett will never forget his tour of the Whaley House. His visit was before the days when sheets of glass kept the public from reaching into the rooms. As he passed the kitchen, he was startled to see the meat cleaver moving. "I reached out my hand to steady it, but it immediately started up again," he confided. This was said to happen so frequently that the curators finally put it away.

The upstairs windows flew open by themselves and set off burglar alarms so often they had to be nailed shut. The day I visited, I was downstairs chatting with a volunteer when two men came racing down the stairs to tell us they had just heard an odd, inexplicable clicking. By the time I got upstairs, the noise had stopped. I secretly thought they were imagining things—until I read that the very sound they described had long been a mystery there.

Others say they've seen the ghost they believe to be Mrs. Whaley. And when music inexplicably floats from the still piano, they attribute it to her.

One curator admitted he'd seen a lovely young woman in vintage dress. "She was unpacking a suitcase," he confided. "Only the top half of her body was visible."

I know who she was: the author of the following poem:

Mad from life's history,
Swift to death's mystery:
Glad to be hurled,
Anywhere, anywhere,
Out of this world.
        —Violet Whaley, August 1885

Violet Eloise Whaley was a tender twenty-two years old on the sunny morning of August 19, 1885. The *San Diego Union* chronicled the horrible events.

Lillie Whaley testified as follows: I reside at Old San Diego. The person lying here is Violet E. Whaley. . . . Last saw her alive around 6 o'clock this morning. . . . Father went down to get his horse, then came up and asked where Violet was. After he went down the second time he opened the back door and called to her.

The Whaley House parlor, where reporters once trooped in to see poor dead Violet after her last desperate act.

Thomas Whaley called out, "Violet, do you want a peach?" His daughter was in the water closet, and she answered him with a gunshot.

Lillie continued.

Mama and I heard the shot. Coming downstairs I found Papa had brought her in, apparently dead. . . . My sister threatened to take her life on the 5th of July this year. Think she was tired of life. She thought no one cared for her and her life was a burden.

Three years earlier, Violet had married a man her parents did not approve of. The newspaper described him as

a worthless fellow, with whom she lived but two weeks. . . . A divorce was procured from her faithless husband, Edson, who had several aliases, and she returned to her maiden name.

One can only imagine the "I told you so's" when the union failed. In a time when divorce was a scandal, the experience must have been shattering. As the newspaper stated, *The marriage blighted her life, and its curse has built her tomb.*

What a powerful moment it must have been for nineteen-year-old Violet when she unpacked her suitcase just weeks after she had filled it in anticipation of a life with her love. The moment was so painful that it imprinted on the room, where it replayed nearly a century later when a curator peered into the bedroom and witnessed it.

The *San Diego Union* lamented the loss of lovely Violet.

Refined and intelligent, and a passionate lover of the beautiful in nature, she also worshiped the arts, and music was her passion. But the piano is now silent, and the guitar will never more wake to her touch.

The article went on to describe how reporters trouped in to see beautiful dead Violet in repose on a "makeshift cot" in the Whaley parlor. The distraught woman had shot herself in the heart.

Violet wrote in her suicide note that her life had been a lie. Now, it seems, her *death* is a lie, hushed up, all but erased from history. Oh, it is there in the library archives. But until I went digging for answers, no one talked about it.

How sad for Violet. And for every other human being who is suffering from depression. Why is it okay to talk about death from cancer but not from suicide?

Violet is forgotten. Is she aware she has been obliterated from memory? Does she want her existence known? Is that why she is so active?

It makes you stop and wonder about the ghostly music that has been attributed to her mother, Anna. Many have reported hearing sounds of tunes rising from instruments with no human hands in sight.

But the piano is now silent, wrote the reporter, *and the guitar will never more wake to her touch.*

Oh, really?

Whaley Legends

The most famous story about the Whaley House concerns Thomas Whaley's first look at the site where the house sits. He and dozens of other folks witnessed the hanging of Yankee Jim, a tall, fair-haired man who had been apprehended for stealing a boat. The chagrined man thought that authorities were only bluffing when they placed the noose around his neck. Surely execution was too severe a punishment.

They were dead serious. The poor man was hanged until the life seeped out of him.

Now, this part of the story has always seemed odd. It is written that as Thomas Whaley watched the horrifying hanging, he thought to himself, I ought to build a house here. And so he did, a huge, two-story brick structure. He put the arch between the parlor and the living room in the exact spot where Yankee Jim was strangled and proudly pointed it out to visitors.

The brutal killing of Yankee Jim is considered to be one of the "nice" little stories that Whaley House historians love to tell. They suggest the house is haunted not just by Yankee Jim but by Thomas Whaley and his wife, Anna, who died of natural causes. Sometimes they mention Thomas Junior, the baby who died in an upstairs bedroom.

Over the years many have claimed to smell Thomas's distinctive Havana cigars or Anna's sweet perfume. There have been sightings of the family's dog, Dolly Varden, who darts down the hall and into the dining room.

Visiting children often claim they see the ghost of Annabelle Washburn. The story goes that the girl was playing with the Whaley children and suffered a crushed windpipe when she ran into a low-hanging clothesline. This account has not been documented. It did, in fact, come from a psychic. I and many others have sifted through the California obituaries in fruitless pursuit of proof of Annabelle's existence. I did, however, find that a builder by the name of Washburn lived in the neighborhood during the right time.

Midnight at The Myrtles

by Kevin Wagner, my skeptical husband

I'm forty-six years old. I stopped believing in Santa Claus a long time ago—not because I wanted to but because the overwhelming preponderance of evidence required it. My evolving concept of time and space made me realize that there were too many chimneys to climb down, too many toys to load into that little sleigh, and just not enough time to visit all the homes in the world.

Similarly, my growing understanding of science and physics has made it increasingly difficult to accept the stories of paranormal phenomena I hear and read about.

This is the mind-set I had when Leslie and I visited The Myrtles, a beautifully preserved antebellum estate situated three miles from St. Francisville, Louisiana, on U.S. 61. This picturesque home was built in 1796 by General David Bradford and was the site of several murders.

The main house at The Myrtles is now divided into two sections, sleeping quarters for guests and a wonderfully restored section that is preserved as a museum and locked every night at 8 P.M., when the caretaker goes home.

It was after 11 P.M. when Leslie and I returned to our room after hours of fascinating exploration. At the bottom of the stairs, next to the locked entrance to the museum, we met the only other guests at the estate: two young couples who had been out celebrating a birthday and drinking a little. We began a humorous and engaging conversation that quickly turned to the subject of hauntings. As we exchanged stories, minutes ticked by and I leaned against the museum door to rest my weary legs. Instead of the support I expected, the door swung open with a creak and I stepped into the doorway of the museum. I immediately jumped back into the entryway. "Oops," I said. "Isn't this supposed to be locked?" Before the words were out of my mouth, the others—Leslie included—were eagerly pushing past me through the open door. As Leslie went by, I heard her whisper, "The ghosts must have opened it." "Coincidence," I whispered back.

The dining room was lavishly decorated with hand-carved woodwork, crystal glass, and fine lace curtains. The dining room table itself was a work of art, at its center a beautiful silver candelabrum sat on a finely crocheted doily.

We sat in the richly crafted chairs around the antique table and continued our conversation. I was in the midst of articulating the scientific foundation for my skepticism to the other men in the group when one of the candles fell from the candelabrum and smacked down loudly on the table. Dead silence followed.

Then I began to laugh, and said in a matter-of-fact tone, "It's probably been years since anyone has actually sat at this table. We obviously bumped it when we sat down."

The other men quickly supported my theory, and as I firmly replaced the candle in its holder we joked about what a fluke it was—except for Leslie, who just smiled.

All the men present were in the construction business and a little on the macho side, myself included. Mike was six-foot-four and weighed about three hundred pounds. He was explaining that it had been years since anything had actually scared him, and John and I were quick to agree. Yes, we were too old and too tough to be scared of some silly ghost nonsense.

Bang! The candle slapped loudly on the table again. I immediately glanced at Mike, whose pale face stood in stark contrast to the numerous tattoos on his upper arms. John's mouth was hanging open, his hands clutching the arms of the chair. Not a word was coming from either of them. I had goose bumps, and the hair on the back of my neck was standing on end. We were three big, tough, really scared men with no idea what the hell to say next.

"So, there's no such thing as ghosts?" Leslie said with a smile.

"It's bull!" said Big Mike.

"Ridiculous!" added John.

"Somebody must have jiggled the table," I offered half-heartedly.

"Okay, let's put the candle back and push away from the table completely," Leslie suggested.

So we did.

Minutes went by. The air seemed heavy and stagnant. The smell of old things pervaded the room—a smell of ancient attics and old trunks filled with memories long forgotten.

"It seems to happen when *you* are talking, Kevin," Leslie whispered, a smirk on her lovely face. "Maybe you should explain again why ghosts are scientifically impossible."

I leaned back in my chair, raised my hands, and said, "Okay, we're all getting a little hysterical here. This is turning into an emotionally driven group hallucination. We are making too much out of a stupid—"

This Louisiana plantation, The Myrtles, is believed to be home to a dozen ghosts.

Myrtle Legends

The Myrtles Plantation Bed & Breakfast
St. Francisville, Louisiana
(225) 635-6277

The Myrtles is believed to be haunted by at least twelve spirits—including Cloey, a slave girl who was caught eavesdropping. When her ear was sliced off in punishment, Cloey baked the plantation owners' two children a birthday cake with a secret ingredient—the deadly oleander that grew outside the house. The children and their mother died, after suffering horrible stomach pains, and the other slaves seized Cloey and hanged her from a tree in the yard. One newlywed couple staying at The Myrtles awoke in the night to see Cloey peering at them. She is said to wear a green head scarf to cover her missing ear.

The ghost of William Winters, a prominent attorney, is also believed to haunt The Myrtles. In 1871, Winters was shot and staggered up the staircase, where he collapsed and died on the seventeenth step. Over the years, many claim to have seen a ghostly reenactment of the murder.

Myrtz the cat snoozes beneath the deadly oleander bush at The Myrtles.

Pow! When the candle hit the table for the third time, it sounded and felt like a rifle shot. It was as if someone had picked it up and slammed it down on its side, flat on the table. It did not tumble or roll or bounce. It just sat there. And so did we. Nobody moved or said a word.

Then Big Mike said, "Oh, man! Do you feel *that?*"

It was as if the cloud of heavy air was being swept from the room by a cool ocean breeze.

In silent union, we all stood up. I replaced the candle a last time, and we pushed our chairs back into place. As we left the room silently, I noticed we were all holding the hands of our wives quite securely.

I have a different mind-set when it comes to ghosts and hauntings these days. I believe there is the possibility of another life, perhaps just a breath away, separated from us by the thinnest of veils: a place inhabited by our ancestors, and a world we shall all someday enter.

The ghost of Cloey oversees The Myrtles.

The Ghosts of Old New Castle

Old New Castle, Delaware: cobblestone streets, tall Colonial homes, enormous trees. The sense of history is so thick, you feel as if you could break off a piece and take it home with you.

Founded by the Dutch as they traveled up the Delaware River, this quaint city was later conquered by the Swedes and then by the British. It is famous for being William Penn's first landing site in North America in 1682.

Named New Amstel before the Duke of York sent a fleet to capture Dutch possessions in the "new world," the town has seen its share of sorrow. It was ravaged by a fire on April 26, 1824. Twenty-two homes and stores were destroyed, but thanks to help from Wilmington firefighters, most were left standing.

It is not surprising Old New Castle is home to so many ghosts. Some believe that at least one of them resides with Bob in his charming two-hundred-year-old house near Battery Park. Bob (who asked to be identified by first name only) is not one to jump to conclusions, but he can't deny the odd occurrences in his home.

In the two decades he's lived there, the puzzling activity has added up. A guitar strums by

A housekeeper was scared away by a ghost in this Old New Castle house.

244

itself. Dishes fly out of cupboards. A window is inexplicably broken from the inside. A mysterious ring appears on the bathroom floor.

It was a sterling silver wedding ring with the initials ESPO engraved on the inside. And it seemed to appear from thin air. Bob found it in the middle of his meticulously cleaned bathroom floor and has never been able to figure out where it came from.

And then there was the time Bob was weeding his yard when he glanced up to see a woman watching him. She appeared about thirty and was clad in a Colonial-style dress. Assuming she was participating in a historic event, he looked away for just an instant. When he looked up again, she had vanished.

Bob doesn't mind the paranormal activity, although it *is* tough to keep a cleaning lady. He came home one day to find the woman who was supposed to be dusting his living room standing across the street. She shakily informed him that she was *not* going back inside that house! She had been cleaning the coffee table and had cleared all the knickknacks to one side. While her back was turned, someone moved everything back to the other side.

"She was really scared," said Bob.

Many other Old New Castle places are said to be haunted, including the David Finney Inn and the Amstel House Museum, a few blocks from Bob's place. These two magnificent brick houses, across the street from each other, were once owned by members of the Finney family and connected by a secret tunnel. Locals believe the same unknown presence lurks at both places. Inexplicable occurrences include windows and doors opening and shutting on their own.

When I stopped in at a nearby deli, the girls working there told me that it, too, was haunted. The water faucet frequently turns itself on and they hear footsteps upstairs when no one is there.

Also in Old New Castle, just a hop, skip, and a jump away, is the Delaware River, where the ghosts of Dutch soldiers have been spotted near the old wooden docks. Some claim to see a *headless* Dutchman marching along the shore.

(Right) When darkness settles on Old New Castle, the spirits like to play.

(Below) Old New Castle's Amstel House is home to a mysterious presence.

Three More of America's Most Haunted

1. The New Orleans French Quarter

In New Orleans, Louisiana, the French Quarter is often referred to as the country's most haunted place. From the infamous LaLaurie House on Royal Street, where slaves were once tortured, to the charming Tea Shop on Bourbon Street, ghosts abound. Spirits seem to lurk in the moss-draped trees and behind every elegant wrought-iron fence.

Louisiana's French Quarter is believed to be crawling with ghosts.

A child of the past gazes from a framed photo displayed in an antiques shop window on the French Quarter's haunted Royal Street.

2. Tombstone, Arizona

This former Wild West city swarms with the ghosts of dance-hall girls and the cowboys who once roamed the area. From Big Nose Kate's, where spirits have been spotted standing in the doorway, to the Bird Cage Theater, where dozens of witnesses have seen long-dead people prance across the stage, Tombstone, Arizona, is a place where the dead don't rest.

3. Garnet, Montana

This gold-mining town was founded in 1895 and was once a hub of activity as hundreds flocked here to make their fortunes. Today it is both literally and figuratively a ghost town, run by the Garnet Preservation Association and the Bureau of Land Management. Honky-tonk music, voices, and laughter have been heard spilling from the vacant Kelly's Saloon, and apparitions of pioneers have been spotted on the empty roads.

Spirits from the past have been seen and heard in Garnet, a preserved ghost town.